All rights reserved worldwide. No part of this publication may be replicated, redistributed, reproduced, reprinted, stored in a retrieval system, or transmitted in any form or by any means (electronic, mechanical, photocopying, recording) or given away in any form or otherwise without prior written permission of the publisher.

For information, write:

admin@AblePublishingOnLine.com

Able Publishing On Line, LLC

165 South Yarrow Street

Lakewood, Colorado 80226 USA

This publication contains the opinions and ideas of its author. It is intended to provide helpful and informative material on the subjects addressed in the publication. It is sold with the understanding that the author and publisher are not engaged in rendering medical, health, or any other kind of personal professional services in the book.

The reader should consult his or her medical, health, or other competent professionals before adopting any of the suggestions in this book or drawing inferences from it.

The author and publisher specifically disclaim all responsibility for any liability, loss, or risk, personal or otherwise, which is incurred as a consequence, directly or indirectly, of the use and application of any of the contents of this book. The publisher has no control over and does not assume any responsibility for third-party websites or their content.

Copyright © 2021 by Able Publishing On Line, LLC

Building Consciousness
by
Expanding Awareness

Ruth Ford Elward

Published 2021

From my Heart to Humanity

Many thanks to my son and grandson,
who light up my heart and give me strength;
to my family and friends; and my editor,
Mary Beth Conlee,
who have all inspired, taught, and helped me
through this journey.

Building Consciousness
by
Expanding Awareness

Ruth Ford Elward

Preface

Much of this book is inspired and organized around the following quote.

Watch your thoughts, for they become words.
Choose your words, for they become actions.
Understand your actions, for they become habits.
Study your habits, for they will become your character.
Develop your character, for it becomes your destiny.

Who actually came up with this particular language is up for grabs. I've seen it credited to Patrick Overton, a 1940s motivational speaker. It's sometimes credited to Buddha. There are many versions, all of which I believe were expanded from an ancient Chinese proverb by Lao Tzu. In reality, I don't know for sure; my research ended at Mr. Overton. I do know that many famous people have quoted this in one form or another: Marianne

Williamson, Gandhi, and Nelson Mandela, to name a few.

Another source of inspiration is Nikola Tesla (1856-1943), and you'll see his name frequently. Tesla was a Serbian-American inventor. He was an electrical and mechanical engineer, and in 1891 he was granted U.S. Patent No. 447,921 for an alternating electric current (AC) generator. He was granted around 300 patents worldwide. I encourage you to check out information on his work and discoveries in the endnotes. I find him inspirational for his focus and discipline; he overcame OCD as he came up with the basis of many of the inventions we enjoy today.[1] He was a futurist with an eidetic memory, spoke seven languages, and often designed and perfected inventions in his imagination.

He once said, "My brain is only a receiver. In the universe there is a core from which we obtain knowledge, strength, and inspiration. I have not penetrated into the secrets of this core, but I know

that it exists."

Introduction

When I was young, I could perceive the subtle energy and feel the emotions of what others were going through. This was so prominent in my life that it set me on a journey of finding out what this life is all about. That, plus the idea that others may have similar experiences and wonder the same thing, motivated me in 1997 to write my first book, *Design Your Intention.*

Nikola Tesla once said, "Life is a rhythm that must be comprehended." I wondered if there was something to understand beyond what we're told as children. Could I learn what life is, or can life only be understood experientially? To me, *life* and *reality* are one in the same—a fluid experience. Reality is a product of consciousness, no matter what plane of existence is occupied. Reality is the inter-related order within a particular space of consciousness. In the following material, *life* and *reality* are used interchangeably.

This book is my idea of how to comprehend the versions of reality and use the rhythm of life so you can choose to walk in peace, compassion, and harmony.

It was prompted by two experiences. The first was a conversation with my grandson after the birth of his first child in late 2018. During this conversation, my grandson said to me, "I wasn't raised with any belief in particular. I feel I should explore religion because that seems to be where most people go, but I don't even know where to start." I'm paraphrasing, but that was the gist of it. I didn't say much then, mainly because to me, religion establishes community but doesn't give a practical understanding of life. I knew there was a way to embrace the fundamental basis of all traditional religions. For me, it's about consciousness, not religion.

As this conversation weighed on me, I wondered what my grandson was really saying and feeling, and what he needed. My interpretation of what he was saying was that he felt a disconnection between his inner and outer worlds. Then it came to me. I thought to myself, "Here is a 20-something who was raised much like a huge number of people in American society—with little understanding of how destiny works from a practical perspective. That it isn't something that just happens; that you create your own destiny day by day." So I began to ponder how to explain this to my grandson—or to any person, for that matter—while addressing the many faces of what religions call God. I believe the right word to represent *God* is whatever makes sense to you.

Then, in early 2019 I was diagnosed with a tumor in my pancreas, and it was cancer. Like everyone else, I had spent much of my life working, getting ahead, traveling, studying, and searching for as many experiences I could, including the elusive mystical/spiritual ones; yet I felt there was still so much more. During that year, I had to take a deeper look at myself and how I could make a contribution through what I had learned and felt I knew about life and the versions of reality that I've experienced. I began by sorting through the essays I have written over the years, and compiling the ones I felt were most relevant for anyone open to the possibility of their truth to receive. My essays include philosophy, mysticism, science, quotes from prominent figures, and links to works by others, with the hope that these resources would open the consciousness for exploring a vast array of possibilities.

Personal development is hardly a linear process. The search for meaning is an existential process. Integrating information, inspiration, and practice spirals throughout a lifetime, coming and going and then coming back around to a deeper understanding. Throughout my journey to learn about life, I found I had a hard time understanding humanity. Then someone shared with me, "The only two things that exist are Love and Thought." That statement led me to understand that the inner state is reflected in the daily outer life, constructing the versions of reality that humanity experiences. The following group of essays highlight some of what I have found to be essential concepts, and attempt to provide you with some mindful practices for organizing and building your consciousness by expanding your awareness.

Contents

Preface..1

Introduction...4

This Incredible Human Experience......................11

Attention: an Easy First Step 18

Choose your words, for they become actions 30

Understand Your Actions, for They Become Habits .36

Karma...39

Awareness and Intention.......................................43

Consciousness 47

Choosing Your Own Reality...................................52

Imagination 65

Habits Reflect Your Character.............................68

Morality...75

Your Character Becomes Your Destiny.....................77

Energy, Frequency, and Vibration 80

Why Do This Work? 98

Technology and Intelligence 100

Enlightenment 106

Practices 108

Nothing to Fear but Fear Itself..........................122

Dealing with Fear..126

Fractals 133

The Holographic Principle 136

The Flower of Life..139

Ready to re-wire your brain? 142

Chakras 145

Entanglement and the Collective Consciousness 154

Conclusion...160

Awaken...165

Questions for the Reader 166

About the Author...172

Endnotes 173

This Incredible Human Experience

I'll start from the beginning: energy is everywhere, and everything is comprised of energy. Energy is not made *of* anything, it is carried *by* something, and there is no physical "essence" of energy. Energy is a term used to describe a trait of matter and non-matter fields. It is the *potential for change.* Energy does not distinguish by race, nationality, walks of life, gender, or religion.

Energy could be referred to as the movement within the Infinite Field from which life exists. This Infinite Field is unconditional, intelligently creative, and powerful; it just IS. Included in it are a series of grids that we generate through our consciousness, collectively. These grids are like a net, going sideways, up, down, and out, out, out... something like the neurons and neural networks in the brain. This Infinite Field contains all that was, is, and ever shall be: all realities and all possibilities. We connect through this Infinite Field of Consciousness.

The intelligence that permeates this Infinite Field has been called the Divine, the Universal Presence, Source, God, etc. and is seen in the way it has, from the beginning, caused the chemical reactions needed to manifest form: the stars, planets, and minerals required for what we call life. The energy within this field can neither be created nor destroyed; just transferred or transformed. It is impersonal and personal. It is unconditional in the way it allows itself to be used by one and all for whatever is desired to be created/manifested.

The power of this intelligence creates limitless possibilities. Your power is to bring the best of those possibilities to life instead of the worst by having trust and faith in what you are offering to the world. How you perceive this intelligence and whether you believe it exists or not will be the foundation of how you experience your version of reality. Reality comes from the value judgements in your mind. Whether you are an atheist and believe there is nothing beyond this physical world, or you believe in someone else's matrix simulation, or you believe in God or Buddha, consciousness is fundamental. From consciousness, your awareness/intent can modify future possibilities of what happens in the physical world.

Within the Infinite Field, energy runs within, through, and around all that exists as we know it—within cells, atoms, electrons, subatomic particles, DNA, RNA, everything. Plants, minerals, animals, everything. Inanimate, animate, everything. We humans color this energy with layers of perceptions from our thoughts and feelings. Perhaps we do so because energy is such an elusive concept, and our carnal mind—what I like to call the little mind—is fond of creating meaning-making scenarios to keep us occupied. The little mind will analyze ad nauseam, looping around the same subject over and over again, causing suffering and separation.

Tesla once said, "...everything we once saw, heard,

read, or learned accompanies us in the form of light particles."[2]

In physics, a photon is a bundle of electromagnetic energy, the basic unit that makes up all light. If you think of consciousness as flow, then light is its substance. Our brains collect photon particles, and we color those particles with our thoughts and feelings, which turn into perceptions, which turn into memories that are stored in the energy outside our physical bodies. The mind exists outside the body within the Infinite Field. Our little mind constantly projects these memories through our thoughts, feelings, and words, turning them into actions. The mind is not the brain, and it is limited by these perceptions of what we've seen, heard, felt, read, and were taught, as well as by our genetic lineage. Repressed or deep-level formations can form as blocked energy in the body where something has been suppressed (i.e. anger, guilt, and hatred), causing dis-ease in the physical body, blocking the mind's "light" and creating chaos in the little mind. The brain is a processor and an accessing device—much like an IP address on the internet—used to retrieve information from the mind.

Helena P. Blavatsky, author of *The Secret Doctrine,* wrote, "The *mind* is a name given to the sum of the states of consciousness grouped under thought, will, and feeling."[3]

If we would take a step back and contemplate the simple truth of this unconditional intelligence in the Infinite Field, maybe we could begin to *see* that which we have accepted as truth from our limited perceptions, and begin to sense the Reality of Oneness that connects us all. Think of the revelation that would be.

> What about the birth of the Universe? Matter is created from the original and eternal energy that we know as Light. It shone, and there appeared stars, the planets, man, and everything on the Earth and in the Universe. Matter is an expression of

infinite forms of Light because
energy is older than it.
                              —Nikola Tesla[4]

Scientists have said we are born of the stars, which is true because the intelligent energy that worked to form the elements not only formed the heavens, but formed us. Every atom in our bodies comes from some star. We are made of stardust; the iron in our blood, the calcium in our bones, and all the other heavy elements in our body were created in super-novic explosions. There is an article from a 1984 *Washington Post* article entitled "<u>The Cosmic Riddle – How Rocks and Stars became Flesh and Blood</u>," by Eugene F. Mallove, an astronautical engineer, that addressed this concept in detail. [5]

If enough people were to embrace the truth of energy, honor the unconditionality of the intelligence enlivening it, and simply give attention and awareness to how we use it, our world would change in an instant. Without this infinite energy field, nothing would exist. No war, no famine, no judgement, no pettiness—because nothing, including us, would exist!

Attention: an Easy First Step

When you think of the word *attention*, you might think of the simple action of observing, of taking notice of something or someone. But for our purposes, the definition and application of the word goes much deeper.

The Western mind, with its strong leaning towards intellect and logic, tends to identify attention with the little mind and thinking. Here, we will use "attention" in that way, as well as in its much wider, multidimensional form. The latter combines the physical act of *passively noticing*, which is our more normal state, with *active noticing*, which takes effort and involves focus, concentration, and alertness.

We live in many worlds at once: a physical world, an emotional world, and a world of thought, each co-existing and often colliding. Being aware that each of these worlds affects us differently yet simultaneously requires active attention, or *mindfulness.*

Active versus passive attention

When you're out taking a leisurely walk, *passive* attention involves noticing the path you are walking on in general, and that you are out for a walk. *Active* attention focuses on where each foot is being placed on the ground, plus a number of other sensory experiences. These other specifics might include a gentle breeze, the smell of flowers, and a dog barking at a cat in a nearby tree, or a memory of a past walk with someone dear to you.

For our purposes, we'll focus on the physical world. A familiar neighborhood sidewalk, a concrete path in a park, or a wide, paved street makes normal, passive attention easy and adequate, whereas a very narrow, winding, rocky, hilly, unfamiliar path requires more active attention, being careful and cognizant of where you place each foot as you go.

In the latter example, your heightened cognizance could be logically construed as purely a matter of safety due to the rocky, hilly nature of the path, and of course, safety would be a concern. However, the definition we are using for active attention in this case is *the state of awareness* or consciousness such deliberate focus can bring.

The good news is that in the beginning, the very act of recognizing that your usual state of attention is passive is the beginning of active attention. It is an easy first step. ***Watch your thoughts, for they become words.***

We think the universe is based on dualities because we see effects but not cause. Thoughts come first, but immediately a feeling is attached to it. We think of our minds as being this all-powerful device, but what is often not comprehended is that there are levels to our mind. We may call them subconscious, conscious, and superconscious; it doesn't matter.

Little mind, higher mind

Personally, I like to keep things as simple as possible and just say we have a little mind and a higher mind. Think of the little mind as what holds most of the past informational data we refer to as knowledge from what we have learned in the form of our perceptions. The little mind includes the thoughts and immediately attaches the feelings about each subject. This is what we use on a daily basis, and what causes the chaos and confusion we experience. The higher mind (sometimes called the higher self) holds the loftier information, the information we can access deep within the Infinite Field, if we can get past the chattering and storytelling the little mind constantly generates.

Here are some examples of people who tapped into the higher mind.

- Edgar Cayce, known as the sleeping prophet, had to sleep or go into a trance to access his higher mind.
- Albert Einstein said, "I am enough of an artist to draw freely upon my imagination.

Imagination is more important than knowledge. Knowledge is limited. Imagination encircles the world." It's said that during a dream, Einstein saw a scenario where he was inspired with the theory of Relativity. The dream showed him that events look different depending on where you're standing because of the time it takes the light to reach your eyes.

- Elias Howe realized what he needed to do to make the lock-stich sewing machine during a dream.

- Dr. James Watson saw a spiral staircase that gave him the idea of a double helix spiral structure for DNA during a dream.

- Niels Henrik David Bohr had a vision in a dream of the nucleus of the atom with electrons spinning around it, like planets going around the sun. This inspired him to dedicate his research to the idea, and he ended up winning a Nobel Prize for his investigation of the structure of atoms and the radiation emanating from them.

Interestingly enough, grasping the possibilities within the Infinite Field requires bypassing or directing the little mind so we can access the higher mind. Think of the Infinite Field as an onion: each layer is a plane of existence. The collective gridwork, your personal gridwork, your reality, the higher mind, as well as past, present, and future limitless possibilities—all that exists in each layer for that plane to experience. Just like the onion, there is a thin film or veil between each layer. The way to access each layer of this onion is through the consciousness. Once one layer of the onion has been experienced and integrated, the next becomes available through the expansion of consciousness that takes place in order to experience, process, and integrate the previous layer. The first layer is the thickest and densest, and requires steady focus and effort to process and integrate. The majority and main focus of this book is to assist in the penetrating, processing, and integrating this first layer of the onion of your experience. However, it also includes material that will nudge you in the direction of the next layer as well.

As we continue, we'll explore ways to access the higher mind—and not just through dreams. But first it's crucial to understand the effects the little mind has on our lives, and how to direct it.

Impact of the little mind

It's important to be aware that we are in the little mind most of the time, and that we construct/attract/manifest from that place. Thoughts in the little mind run rampant, constantly creating scenarios or stories based on past perceptions. This little mind aspires to nothing higher than a hostile, self-centered state of existence. It lacks control and direction. Did you know that the average person generates 60,000 to 80,000 thoughts a day? The thought generated from the little mind "shows how our experience emerges through our senses and how our bodies are not just visible objects, but also sense-making visual subjects," as Vivian Sobchack wrote in *Carnal*

Thoughts.[6] Each of those thought scenarios carry an amount of energy with them. This energy sits, like infinitesimal formations collecting and clogging up the consciousness.

The solution is simple: slow down. You will never be able to completely turn off the little mind. However, there are ways to direct it that free up the clogged energy, like meditation, visualization, contemplation, and breathing, all of which can produce a calming effect. Freeing the energy of our perceptions and allowing space for them to transform or be released generates peace.

Simply sit in a comfortable position with your back erect. Close your eyes and breathe *slowly*. The in breath should expand and fill the belly, and the outbreath should move the belly toward the spine. The outbreath should be longer than the in breath. Be mindful of the *slow* in and out of breathing. Do not allow any anxiety to pace your breath. Gently move back to the breath if you find your mind wandering to the grocery list or what your friend meant by that comment.

If your mind continues to wander, try touching your thumb and the tip of the index finger of each hand on the breath, then move the thumb to the tip of the middle finger on the next breath, and so on. You do not need to count your breaths. By touching your fingers at each breath, you occupy your mind while staying focused. If touching your fingers doesn't work for you, there is another way to occupy the mind: simply come up with one syllable that has no meaning, and inwardly say that over and over again. This will keep the little mind occupied while staying focused on the breath itself. If you do this practice for 20 minutes in the morning and 20 minutes at night for a month, you will be surprised at how calm and peaceful your thoughts will become. You'll also find you will listen more, and the words you choose to express yourself will be different.

When you meditate, think of your mind as an ocean.

Little air bubbles come up to the surface from various depths of the ocean; these are merely the energy of all those thoughts and the feelings attached to them. Some have firmer formations from being repressed. These bubbles can cause an emotional response. Just allow it. You do not need to know what the content is specifically; just allow the emotions to bubble up, float away, and dissipate. You are the observer. If you focus on the content, you are giving permission to the little mind to play out the content over and over again, looping itself and keeping you from moving beyond it. The looping of content in the mind is called the suffering state. The difference between being an observer and being a witness is that being an observer is a practice of awareness that is done in the mind, while witnessing is experienced while in an expanded state of consciousness.

Ishmael Tetteh, a mystic from Ghana, Africa, describes it in the following way: "The job of water in the ocean is the entire ocean. The water in the ocean can choose to see itself as a drop of water, having its own existence within the ocean. If that drop of water becomes a witness, it sees that it is one with the entire ocean, or it can choose to see its connectedness to the ocean."

Every day we are constantly bombarded within and without. Technology, with all its helpfulness, also leads us to distraction. We are pulled in many directions. We are told how we should think and feel, what we should desire, and how we should act. It's our responsibility to take ourselves back, to be aware, to consciously experience our life and ourselves within that reality—and to be something more for doing so.

And that requires active attention. I highly recommend going to https://www.breathingroom.com/free-meditations-english. There are numerous free videos there; one about three minutes long is on meditation. The offerings on this site are guided meditations. One in particular is called Soul Sync, and is about 17 minutes long. The Soul Sync meditation will help you touch upon your real self—the self that is greater than what you see in the mirror.

I will mention two things here briefly that may help you in expanding your awareness to a broader perspective of your potential capabilities.

The first is *Transurfing in 78 Days: A Practical Course in Creating Your Own Reality.* This book contains a mental technique to help you master the quieting of the mind. It was written by quantum mechanics physicist Vadim Zeland. The second is to research courses that can teach you how to "see" blindfolded. I was taught by Mihaela Istrati of InfoVision Academy.[7] These courses teach the ability to perceive visual information without using your eyes.

Now on to the guts of what is needed to understand the practical side of reality…

Choose your words, for they become actions

Words are the manifestation of our thoughts combined with the energy of our feelings.

Have you ever had a thought like, "I'm angry with so and so because they did so and so," and swore to yourself that you were not going to tell anyone, you were just going to release it—and then it comes spilling out in a conversation with someone? Of course you have; we all have. It doesn't make you bad; it's just a simple example of how often we aren't in control of ourselves, and how

Thoughts + Feelings = Words.

"Watch your thoughts" means to actively pay attention to their origins and their consequences. This awareness allows your thoughts to serve you rather than you unconsciously serving your thoughts.

Here's another thing that happens often: you hear something good or derogatory about something or someone and unconsciously accept it as truth. This magnetizes other like-minded thoughts, and when that subject or person comes up in conversation, your thoughts reference what you accepted as truth along with any other like-minded thoughts, and you respond from that perspective: a completely unconscious process.

The power of words

 A perfect example of the power of words as I write this is how politics has evolved into something that bullies, demonizes, and scapegoats as a norm, turning a blind eye to unethical and immoral actions. The "us against them" attitude has become dominant as lies are told and destructive energy permeates our country.

Words can be glorious. Words can empower. Words can cause war, words can destroy, words can manipulate, and words can and will influence the minds and hearts of people.

Savvy marketers learned this a long time ago, but it is being taken to new heights now, especially by appealing to our fears. You have to decide the truth for yourself. Will you direct your own thoughts and words, or just repeat what you hear?

Words have physical impact, too. In the 1990s, <u>Dr. Masuru Emoto</u>[8] conducted a series of experiments observing the physical effect of words, prayers, and music on the crystalline structure of water. He exposed the water to these messages and then photographed its molecular makeup. The photos of the water given positive words or graceful music was far more symmetrical and aesthetically pleasing than those stamped with dark, negative phrases or chaotic sounds. I bring this up because 75% of all biological tissue is water—including the human body. What messages do you give yourself and others?

Choose your words, for they become actions. The words you speak are mini representations of yourself. If you find yourself regularly criticizing, belittling, judging, and pointing out flaws in others or yourself, it's time to look inside.

Those words are a reflection of what you carry in your mind and radiate out through your energy field and actions. If your thoughts, feelings, and words are typically unconscious, then of course your actions will lack awareness as well. For example, if someone is judgmental about you and expresses it to you, you likely feel wronged. How do you respond?

- Do you go on the attack?
- Are you vengeful? Are you a bully, needing to win no matter what or at any cost?
- Are you more concerned about how you might look to others, or are you more concerned about saying and doing the right thing?
- Do you look for someone to join you in your outrage, because having numbers on your side makes you right, or better than the one perpetrating the judgement?

Or say you have done the same to someone else. Somewhere inside, did you consciously know that those words would be hurtful? Did you catch yourself and create the action of apologizing for the words spoken? When you know you've caused pain, do you ask for forgiveness, whether it be out in the open or within yourself?

Without the giving and receiving of forgiveness in your life, the motion of moving beyond that which holds you back is thwarted. It's a small thing with great effect to, before going to sleep at night, sincerely move into a state of gratitude for all that you've been given for the day, ask for forgiveness from anyone you may have caused pain, and forgive anyone that has caused you pain. You don't have to be specific, for there is no way to know all the people you may have hurt; just hold true forgiveness and contrition in your heart.

Your thoughts and feelings generate your words. They show who you are, and have remarkable impact on yourself, others, and the world. Use them consciously.

Understand Your Actions, for They Become Habits

Thoughts attract feelings, which lead to words and then to actions, creating your habitual state and disposition. Your actions represent you in the world.

Words + Actions = Habitual State

It's a short step from actions to habits. A habit is a settled or regular tendency or practice. When we do the same things frequently, responding in the same way over and over again, they become habits. These habits become unconscious reactions, triggered by a deeply ingrained perspective.

Albert Einstein is widely credited with the saying, "The definition of insanity is doing the same thing over and over again, but expecting different results."

When we use active attention, we have the means

to look at our habits and what they say about us, and propel us toward change if we so choose.

How to change habits

There is a book I recommend, a *New York Times* bestseller called *Atomic Habits: An Easy and Proven Way to Build Good Habits and Break Bad Ones*, by James Clear. He makes the point that many people think they lack motivation to change when what they really lack is clarity (or active attention).

Clear makes a statement that I agree with, and that is, "Every action is a vote for the type of person you wish to become." You can download a free chapter on his website.[9]

Accountability

Actions have consequences. In the world in which we live, cause and effect exists, and therefore every action has a result. You may not see them today or tomorrow or next year, but the consequences of your every habit, action, feeling, and thought are always there, and in the end, you are responsible for them.

Who's to say that the mishaps that befall us aren't linked to the energy we have misused? There is a means to help us understand the balancing of the energy we use, and that concept is *karma*.

Karma

What is karma? Karma is the result we have set in motion and the effects we will reap from those actions: karma is reaping the harvest of the seeds our actions have planted. It is based on your intention and the actions those intentions trigger.

Many people think karma means fate—something inevitable. It is not. It's the effect of not taking responsibility for the right use of the life energy given to us.

Karma comes from the Sanskrit word for *deed*. The <u>Hindu definition</u> is:

1. A mental or physical action;
2. The consequence of a mental or physical action;
3. The sum of all consequences of the actions of an individual in this or some previous life;

4. The chain of cause and
    effect in the world of
    morality.[10]

Each individual's karma is created by that person's *samskaras*: the impressions, tendencies, and possibilities present in consciousness that have arisen through one's actions and thoughts, including those of earlier births. The sum total of *samskaras* form the person's character.[11]

This possibility directs one's behavior and steers the motives for all present and future thoughts and deeds. Thus every karma is the seed for further karma. Its fruits are reaped in the form of joy or sorrow, according to the type of thought or action enacted.

Every human being creates their own limitations through their past thoughts and actions. Having formed these tendencies, we have the option of continuing to follow those tendencies or to resist and change them.

In the Buddhist sense, karma is defined as "the universal law of cause and effect." Andre Bareau writes in *Die Religionen Indiens*,

> The deed (karma) produces a fruit under certain circumstances; when it is ripe then it falls upon the one responsible... Since the time of ripening generally exceeds a lifespan, the effect of actions is necessarily one or more rebirths, which together constitute the cycle of existence.[12]

Polarity is something with two opposing but related qualities. Think of the board of a seesaw in constant motion. The board moves up and down as we ponder the differences between choices to be made. The state of attachment toward either side causes the up or down motion as we grapple with the forces naturally opposing each other. In other words, with each action, you are either moving towards or away from something. It is believed that in doing so, we accumulate the consequences of those choices, which is karma.

Think of a plumb line running down the midpoint of the seesaw. This midpoint is where the sides are equal but opposite, existing at the same time. Neither side has a charge for the outcome; it's a place of neutrality. Professor Alan Woodward shows us a mirror of this in describing _quantum superposition_. "When an electron is in superposition, it is both up and down at once; it is a complex combination of both. Only when it is measured does it drop out of superposition and adopt one position or the other."[13]

When we can stay in the midpoint between the up or down movement, we become the observer. This is the non-duality point of both the inner and outer. Your choices can reflect as a mode of either an observer or a witness, for those choices are the movement of energies that influence your destiny. The hard part about choices is living with them. In order to find balance, you must first have awareness of both sides of any issue, and then hold that point of neutrality between the two so that choices can be made with mindfulness.

Awareness and Intention

Awareness is the state of being awake to what you are experiencing. It comes from attention. Awareness encompasses knowledge or perception of something that can lead to action. Awareness is being conscious, cognizant, informed, and alert. It is the state or ability to know, feel, and perceive, or to be sensible of events, objects, or patterns.

It can be said that thoughts are born in awareness and pass from awareness. Well-functioning awareness evaluates and contains unstable thoughts before they cause harm. The purpose of awareness is to offer hope and more. By translating awareness into actionable items, we can change behavior, habits, and even beliefs.

Start increasing your awareness by looking at yourself objectively and asking trusted friends to describe you to verify your objectivity. Keep a journal; write down your plans, goals, and priorities. Self-reflect every day through meditation, visualization, contemplation, and other mindful habits.

Self-awareness is focusing on yourself and how your thoughts, feelings, words, and actions do or do not align with your internal values. It helps you to correctly understand how others perceive you.

Knowing our internal states, preferences, and intuition increases our self-awareness and aids not only in understanding our own behaviors and feelings, but also those of others. Self-awareness is a thinking skill that focuses our ability to accurately evaluate performance and behavior so we can respond appropriately to different social situations. Self-awareness is a key to self-realization.

Intention is much like desire. Intention and desire are the mental and emotional components of your pathway: the aim/bow (intention), the goal/target (desire), and the accelerant/arrow (passion).

Consider the bow and arrow moving towards a target: whether or not they connect to the target has to do with how strong your passion is to make the right choices along the way.

By setting an intention, you send a message that you intend to attract and direct into your life, rather than allowing the day or week to just happen. Intention is the aim fueled by the passion you hold to accomplish the goal. It is the determination, objective, or plan to do a specific thing. For example, every year we make New Year resolutions. We set an intention like losing weight, and we plan on accomplishing this by working out every day and eating more nutritionally. How successful we are is determined by visualizing the end goal in the mind's eye: by focusing our daily attention on the actions required to achieve what we desire. To do this, we have to be aware of any thoughts, feelings, and actions that may sabotage reaching that goal.

An intention is a directed impulse of consciousness

that contains the seed form of that which you aim to
create.

–<u>Deepak Chopra</u>[14]

Consciousness

A critical part of choosing your reality is to become aware of your internal and external existence so that you can alter it. This awareness can be defined as intelligence. When you focus your awareness, you become conscious of the content. One way of describing consciousness is *the intelligent movement of awareness*. This movement can be the movement of atoms within a material structure, or the thought waves of a genius.

There are many levels of consciousness. In 1995, David R. Hawkins, M.D., Ph.D. wrote a book called *Map of Consciousness*; in 2020 it was updated to *The Map of Consciousness Explained*. This book can help you understand and identify where your awareness is in any given moment. Hawkins identified 1,000 points within the ranges of consciousness.

Does consciousness pervade the universe?

One of science's most
challenging problems is a
question that can be stated
easily: Where does
consciousness come from? In
his new book, *Galileo's Error:
Foundations for a New Science
of Consciousness*, philosopher
Philip Goff considers a radical
perspective: What if
consciousness is not something
special that the brain does, but
is instead a quality inherent to
all matter? It is a theory known
as "panpsychism," and Goff
guides readers through the
history of the idea, answers
common objections (such as
"That's just crazy!"), and
explains why he believes
panpsychism represents the
best path forward.
— Gareth Cook[15]

Panpsychism is defined as a doctrine or belief that everything material, however small, has an element of individual consciousness. This is not a new theory. In the 16th century, the Italian philosopher Francesco Patrizi coined the word *panpsychism*, deriving it from the two Greek words *pan* (all) and *psyche* (soul or mind).

In fact, according to <u>Wikipedia</u>, "Panpsychism is one of the oldest philosophical theories, and has been ascribed to philosophers including Thales, Plato, Spinoza, Leibniz, William James, Alfred North Whitehead and Galen Strawson."[16]

Basically, <u>consciousness</u> is "sentience or awareness of internal or external existence. It may be 'awareness', or 'awareness of awareness', or self-awareness. There might be different levels or orders of consciousness, or different kinds of consciousness, or just one kind with different features." [17]

Consciousness and awareness are somewhat synonymous. *Consciousness* is associated with an innate intelligence that brings about an understanding of what you are aware of, whereas *awareness* depends on your sensory apparatus. Awareness is a result of the interface of information between your sensing apparatus and the intelligence contained in your consciousness. When you have observed something, the 'you' that has observed it is the mind, albeit the little mind. When you are in an expanded state, you are no longer in the little mind; instead, you are experiencing from a witness state of consciousness, the higher mind.

A rock, a tree, or an animal may observe a particular event but remain unaware, or partly aware, of what it has observed, depending on its level of consciousness. A human being in the same circumstance will have a different level of awareness from observing the same event, responding differently because of his or her greater consciousness.

I would like to quote from a 2018 article in *Nature*, this one by Christof Koch: "What is Consciousness?" It considers Integrated Information Theory, which investigates the consciousness of systems. <u>He states</u>,

> The theory begins with the observation that when you are conscious of something, many different parts of your brain have access to that information. If, on the other hand, you act

unconsciously, that information
is localized to the specific
sensory motor system
involved.[18]

Consciousness is the state of awareness, while

awareness is the presence or the state of knowing.

So the difference between consciousness and

awareness is the processing of the information.

Consciousness experiences awareness.

Awareness processes information.

Consciousness processes awareness.

Choosing Your Own Reality

> Reality exists only for a single
> moment like a frame on a film
> role. So, only the immediate
> impression of reality, the
> illuminated frame, is ever real.
> Everything else is virtual, the
> past, and future...To compose
> reality means to choose the film
> roll and determine the direction
> in which the frame is
> moving...You have to compose
> reality ahead of time. You can't
> do it from the current frame.
> — Vadim Zeland

We often hear the phrase, "You create your own reality." This can be thorny to understand. For instance, you might ask, "If you get cancer, did you somehow create that?"

I'll use myself to answer this question. Basically, *yes*. You think, "Is she nuts? Who would want to create such a thing?" Well, we do a lot of things unconsciously, so hear me out. The weakest area of my body must be the pancreas, so that's where the cells couldn't hold a harmonic vibration with the

rest of the body and fell prey to overproducing cells.
This would have taken place over a long period of
time, through the way I responded to events in my
life—holding pent up anger, anxiety, worry, and
stress, causing disharmony in the body's vibration.

Now, I am not taking into consideration, the impact
of past lives karma that could be impacting my
present situation. Past life karma influences are not
an easy concept to explain, let alone understand.
We often ask ourselves, why did this happen to me?
With all the suffering and heinous acts going on
worldwide, it makes this concept even more
difficult to comprehend. So all I'll say is there are
books specifically written on this concept of past
lives and karma. You might want to take the time to
explore them, if this is of interest to you.
What I believe without taking past life karma into
consideration, in my case is, what I couldn't let go
of, transform, or express in appropriate ways, was
held long enough to disrupt the body's natural
ability to combat the overproduction of cells.

The next logical step would be, "If you think you caused the cancer, you should be able to cure, or at least, control the cancer yourself." Again, my answer is *yes*, because our bodies have a tremendous capacity to heal if a harmonic healing vibration is held long enough to affect that which has manifested. It took years for the tumor to form, and could take some time for this to resolve. You can only affect something in the present moment. You cannot change the present moment, but you can use it to affect a future present moment. The universe will rearrange itself for you around the clear, passionate vision of reality you hold.

As Henry Ford said, "Whether you think you can or think you can't, you're right."

Think of yourself as a farmer. You've prepared the field and planted a seed. You must now allow the sun, water, and earth to act upon it. You must let go and be patient so the forces of the universe can act. When the seed germinates, grows, and bears fruit, you celebrate. However, along the way, things happen—maybe not enough sunlight or too much water—and the results aren't ideal. What do we do when we don't get what we want? We blame someone or something through our thoughts, feelings, words, and actions.

I am not saying, I celebrate my cancer, but I am taking responsibility for it rather than blaming the Divine or wallowing in self-pity or fear. I choose to see the Divine as benevolent in my reality, not as uncaring. How I live with or without cancer is what I find to be important. I don't allow the up or down or oscillation of thoughts and emotions to take over and sidetrack me from my version of reality.

The seesaw (or pendulum) of my thoughts, feelings, words, and actions over a period of time—maybe even from a past life or lives, or even from collective reality—may have all come into play when this cancer was formed. It doesn't matter which one/s contributed to its manifestation.

Reality is whatever you create with your mind from what you came in with and what you've accumulated here. Reality is transitional, and mine happens to include free will, or freedom of choice. I observe the event, become aware of what is being offered, and ask for Divine's intervention when I cannot see clearly.

There are many ways we can perceive our reality. I'd like to focus on three: the observer, the role of mirroring, and the role of identity.

The observer

There are two things Steve Jobs and I have in common. The first is the same kind of tumor in our pancreas; it's called a neuro-endocrine tumor, and is fairly rare. The second thing is the book *Autobiography of a Yogi*, by Paramhansa Yogananda, a Hindu monk (a book I heartily recommend you read). This was the only book Jobs had on his iPad when he passed away. This book was also the last gift he gave to his family and friends at his funeral. Yogananda saw life as a motion picture moving before his eyes. When he occupied the place of the one watching the movie, he found he could ride the waves of life with much more awareness and less drama. He said,

> A man who sits in a cinema watching simultaneously the image on the screen and the imageless beam of light overhead knows it is the film, and not the beam, that is the direct cause of the changing pictures of shadows and light.

Mirroring

Interestingly, Vadim Zeland (the author of *Transurfing in 78 Days*) holds a similar view about seeing life as a motion picture, but he goes into detail about how to utilize that information to create your own reality, and he adds the concept of mirroring.

My understanding of Zeland's mirroring effect is that the thoughts, feelings, words, and actions we project into the world are reflected back to us by others or by experiences. This mirroring can assist the objectivity of self, increasing awareness of what may need to change or heal through the journey to self-realization.

For example, say you have a friend who frequently irritates you by being hypercritical—they find it necessary to constantly correct you or others over perceived mistakes. The mirror effect tells you that whether you outwardly do the same or not, inwardly, somewhere you hold judgement as well. Your judgmental nature is being reflected back to you by your friend, and that's why you react to it. Once you are aware that you are reacting, accept your participation in the process, and are open to its insight, you can reflect on the cause within you that creates your reaction. If you understand the cause, you will be able to let go of it and no longer have a reaction to such behavior. You will find that wondrously, you don't react to how your friend deals with what she judges to be mistakes. Who has changed?

Zeland's mirroring shows who and what you are attracting or magnetizing to yourself, so you can see (and thus choose) how you are perceiving your reality. Going deeper, let's discuss what unconditional means here. The only one you can change is yourself. It is fruitless to think you can change another's behavior. When you can see the divinity—that point within another that we all have—and focus on that and not on the other person's behavior—for we are all evolving—you will touch upon unconditional love.

I agree with both Yogananda and Zeland, for I have used techniques like these to navigate my life. In perceiving life as a movie, you become the projectionist—the observer. From the present frame of film, you can choose to create the content of future frames in your movie, thus choosing your reality.

Understanding your identity

We create our identity through our consciousness from the input we have coming at us from all directions as we grow up. This input creates impressions upon our consciousness from which we make decisions about who and what we are in life. There are also sub-aspects to our identity that have to do with the thoughts and feelings influencing the decisions being made about our identity. In order to get the most positive outcome as our consciousness expands in life, we have to understand not only what identity we're manifesting *from* but also the sub-aspects affecting it. All that we think, feel, speak, and do is filtered unconsciously through that identity.

Think of a boy growing up in a traditional household where boys do certain things and girls do others. The roles are laid out in front of them, but somewhere deep inside the young boy, he feels different. As time goes by, he realizes he feels more joy during the times he shares with his sisters and what they do rather than what he shares with his brothers. After a time, when it becomes 'inappropriate' for him to continue to play games and share in his sister's antics, he becomes pushed into more manly behaviors. He becomes unhappy, confused, and angry. He realizes something in him isn't the way he was taught he should be; he begins to see himself as more feminine, and wants to change his identity to match what he feels. When he accepts this as his identity, his reality begins to change. As he accepts this, he surrounds himself with others who do too, and he is no longer unhappy, confused, or angry. Instead, he feels he has found a place in the world that matches his identity.

Another example: a woman grows up in a traditional household, taught that women take care of the children and home. In her later years, she feels she has missed something, that the role of housewife isn't enough. She has experienced satisfaction from it and loves her family, but she needs more. There seems to be an empty space in her that needs to be filled. She decides it's time to have a career. She goes back to school and becomes a real estate agent. Now she feels much more complete. She still has her traditional role as a wife and mother, but she has expanded it to encompass an identity of a businesswoman—someone who helps others through the trying, exhausting process of finding or selling a home.

Or remember Richard Alpert. In the early 1960s, Alpert, along with Timothy Leary, conducted research on the therapeutic effects of psychedelic drugs at Harvard University. At the time this was not illegal, but it did cause controversy and led to his dismissal from Harvard in 1963. Years later, he found a path of spirituality and took that on as his identity for the rest of his life. He became known as Ram Das, and founded the charitable organizations Seva Foundation and the Hanuman Foundation. He spent his life giving talks, retreats, and fundraisers for charitable causes.

These are a few examples of how an identity can be used to create or expand our reality—how we can modify our identities when they don't serve us, and how they can propel us or hold us back.

If you can be honest enough to identify what you consider your identity to be, you can change or modify it depending on how it serves you. You will also need to identify some of the sub-aspects of your identity that propel you forward, and those that hold you back. Sounds simple—and it will be, if you're not too attached to the current aspects of your present identity. We'll deal with the fear that may surround doing this a bit later.

Being able to work with how you see your identity is an important mechanism in understanding how you perceive your own reality.

Versions of reality

Because we are all connected, we share a collective reality. But you can also choose your own reality within it. Why would you want to choose your own reality rather than staying a victim of the collective reality? The reasons are simple: to be free, to expand, to learn, and to grow. How do you do that? By awakening and expanding your level of consciousness.

I believe there are more realities to experience beyond what is called enlightenment, or maybe they are different facets of enlightenment—I hold great passion for experiencing these as I learn to not effort and just be. I have touched into the one beyond where I live now for periods of time, and then I return to my present version of reality.

This book was complete with everything I wanted to say when I was shown a video. I was flabbergasted, for this video talks about the versions of reality I've moved in and out of over my life. The video is of Krishnaji, a mystic philosopher and co-founder of O&O Academy, an international philosophy and meditation school in southern India. In the video, he describes Divine Will and Free Will in relation to four versions of reality with great eloquence.[19]

Imagination

It's funny: every time I think or write the word *imagine* or *imagination*, I think of John Lennon's song, *Imagine*. His lyrics are profound; if you haven't listened to it recently, I suggest you do.

Albert Einstein said,

> Imagination is more important than knowledge. For knowledge is limited to all we know and understand, while imagination embraces the entire world, and all there ever will be to know and understand.

We've covered a significant amount of information here, but we haven't added the ingredient of imagination. Imagination is yet another practice, for imagination fuses and unifies. In order for imagination to ignite our thoughts, we need to embrace what imagination is all about: seeing clearly exactly what we desire, and moving all our energy towards it (not with a stranglehold, but with clear vision), while at the same time allowing the universe to re-arrange itself around what we desire, as if we just planted a seed in the ground.

Dr. Murray Hunter of the University of Malaysia Perlis defines imagination as:

> The ability to form mental images, phonological passages, analogies, or narratives of something that is not perceived through our senses. Imagination is a manifestation of our memory, and enables us to scrutinize our past and construct hypothetical future scenarios that do not yet but could exist.[20]

Our life is limited only by our imagination and our dreams. People tend to think of dreaming as "not real," without realizing that what we dream and imagine creates our reality. We can only go as far as we can imagine. As Tao de Haas wrote,

> The ability to imagine things pervades our entire existence. It influences everything we do, think about and create. It leads to elaborate theories, dreams and inventions in any profession from the realms of academia to engineering and the arts.

Ultimately, imagination
influences everything we do,
regardless of our profession.[21]

There is a difference between thinking and imagining. Thought is form created in the mind, rather than the act or power of forming a mental image of something not present to the senses or never before wholly perceived in reality. Imagination is the engine that drives creativity. Imagining is one of the keys to human existence. Without imagination, we couldn't function emotionally, our memories wouldn't work, and we would lack the capacity to travel forwards and backwards in time. Our imagination makes us unique as a species.

Habits Reflect Your Character

Habits are formed by repetition. Repetition is essential because it reflects the consistent patterning of how an individual lives. Habits are a sequence of actions that are done repeatedly, like making your bed every morning, brushing your teeth, or waking up at 6 am to exercise. Because they are routine, they in turn form what we call qualities of *character.* The observable characteristics these actions reflect are those of discipline, self-control, and respect for oneself.

Repetitive actions → Character

Character is defined by Merriam-Webster as "the mental and moral qualities distinctive to an individual; the way someone thinks, feels, and behaves: someone's personality; a set of qualities that are shared by many people in a group, country, etc."[22]

The character of a person, group, or country

consists of the qualities that make them as distinct from other people or places.

A person's character is shown by how they think, act, and feel about life. A person with good character thinks, acts, and feels in a way that aligns with commonly accepted "good" traits, like being honest, respectful, responsible, fair, compassionate, and humble. One other essential good trait is *integrity*. To have integrity is to conduct one's life with strong moral principles and core values as a guide.

Michael Josephson[23] of the Josephson Institute of Ethics posted the following in 2015.

> Character – What is It and Why Is It Important?
>
> On its face, "character" is a morally neutral term. Every person, from iconic scoundrels like Hitler and saints like Mother Teresa, have a character. We use the term *character* to describe a person's most prominent attributes; it is the

sum total of the features and
traits that form an individual's
nature.

To say a person has a good
character, or even to admire a
person's character, does not
require that they are perfect,
but it does mean we think this is
a good person worthy of trust
and admiration.

So when we say someone has
good character, we are
expressing the opinion that his
or her nature is defined by
worthy traits like integrity,
courage, and compassion.
People of good character are
guided by ethical principles even
when it's physically dangerous
or detrimental to their careers,
social standing, or economic
well-being. They do the right
thing even when it costs more
than they want to pay.

No one is born with good
character; it's not a hereditary
trait. And it isn't determined by
a single noble act.

Character is established by
conscientious adherence to
moral values, not by lofty
rhetoric or good intentions.

Another way of saying that is "character is ethics in action."

Anne Frank, the 13-year-old victim of Nazi persecution, said in her diary, "The formation of a person's character lies in their own hands." I have no doubt that she was right. Of course, efforts by parents, teachers, and others to instill these values are very important. They can have a great deal of influence on the values a child adopts, but we must never underestimate the role of choice (and accountability for making that choice) in the formation of character.

Thus, character is both formed and revealed by how one deals with everyday situations as well as extraordinary pressures and temptations. Like a well-made tower, character is built stone by stone, decision by decision.

The way we treat people we think can't help or hurt us—like housekeepers, waiters, and secretaries—tells more about our character than how we treat people we think are important. How we behave when we think no one is looking or when we

don't think we will get caught
more accurately portrays our
character than what we say or
do in service of our reputations.

In studying our habits, we understand our character and can make adjustments through giving attention to our thoughts, feelings and our words, and finally our actions. We must not allow repetitive destructive actions to become habits, but instead consciously create our character.

Your character reflects your nation, and vice versa

I find this particularly interesting because the individuals within a society reflect the character of a nation. A society takes on traits when enough individuals become so numb to what is being pressed upon them that they blindly accept the unacceptable. This attests to the power of our various forms of media and technology, and how much we need to bring active attention to bear on them.

As I write this in 2020, it appears that the moral compass of American society is being manipulated into accepting the unacceptable as the norm, making it somehow right or moral. A marked inability to get along with others or abide by societal rules is called psychopathy or sociopathy.

I find it impossible to talk about individual and collective character without discussing the spirit of an individual or nation. Jason Evans defines *spirit* as:

> 1. The nonphysical part of a person which is the seat of the emotions and character; the soul.
> 2. Those qualities regarded as forming the definitive or typical elements in the character of a person, group or nation, or in the thought and attitudes of a particular period.[24]

We are in a tenuous period right now, and "we the people" must decide if we want this tumultuous period in history to define us as a nation. The only way to change the direction

we're going in is to change ourselves
individually.

Morality

Any discussion of character includes the concept of morality. What is morality, and why is it important? Morality attempts to discern what is *good, bad, right,* or *wrong* in human character and behavior. A moral person follows principles to choose right conduct and good character. The result of choosing the right and good almost always benefits others first, rather than self.

Two associated and often confused terms are *immoral*, which means to intentionally ignore moral standards; and *amoral*, which refers to a person who is unconcerned with the rightness or wrongness of their action at all.

There are three sources which determine the morality of any act: intention, moral object, and consequences.

Intention. The intention is the purpose or goal for which the act was chosen. It is not moral to intend a good end but achieve it through immoral means.

Moral object. The moral object is the end by which the act itself, by its very nature, is directed. Nothing can transform an intrinsically evil act into a moral act. You control which acts you choose. If an act is intrinsically evil, your only choice is to choose a different type of act—one that is moral.

Consequences follow from intention and action. A particular objective act is chosen for a particular subjective purpose and results in specific consequences. The good or bad consequences of the chosen act are part of our morality in so far as these can be reasonably anticipated by the person at the time the act is chosen.

You are choosing your reality through the thoughts, feelings, actions, and habit that make up your character. Is your reality a moral one? And if it isn't, what does that mean for your life or your destiny?

Your Character Becomes Your Destiny

Destiny is not pre-ordained. It is not fated in that it can't be changed; of course destiny can be changed, because we have free will—unless we give that free will away. Destiny is that which you're meant to do through active attention and conscious decisions. *Destiny* is what happens when you commit to learning, taking chances, and evolving, while *fate* is what happens when you don't take responsibility for your life and hand over control to other people and circumstances.

Destiny is something we can actively shape and alter. Qualities such as courage, compassion, willpower, and patience all help to mold your destiny. Destiny is intimately connected to our ultimate life path. *When we choose to step up and take responsibility for our lives, then we are actively shaping our destiny* instead of leaving our lives to fate.

Character → Destiny

Ask yourself, "What do I want the most in life?" Freedom, peace of mind, or maybe love? Then direct all your energy towards it. Remember that happiness can only be found in the present moment.

> Your destiny is being created
> every day, it's being created
> right now, there is not a road
> map already designed for you;
> you are the designer, you create
> your life as you live it.
>
> Today, you are experiencing the
> literal reality of past ways of
> thinking, and to create a future
> for yourself that is one that you
> want or would choose, you can
> do this by paying attention to
> the thoughts that take up most
> of your bandwidth now and
> direct these thoughts or "train
> of thought" in the direction of
> your goals, wants and/or
> desires.
>
> Change your thinking, change
> your life, and create your
> destiny.
> —Gary DiGrazia, Jr.[25]

And now, additional material that will nudge you towards the next layer.

Energy, Frequency, and Vibration

"If you want to find the secrets of the
universe,
think in terms of energy, frequency, and
vibration."

–Nikola Tesla

Everything is energy. But where did it come from and how does it connect us? In order to discuss oneness and connection, we have to explore where science, mysticism, and philosophy intersect. We begin by exploring energy's vibration, frequency, and electromagnetic fields.

Everything in the universe is made up of energy vibrating at different frequencies. *Vibration* is the motion of oscillation in alternating opposite directions, either randomly or in a pattern from a position of equilibrium. Through the disturbance, vibration causes waves that radiate through space, carrying energy from one location to another.

Frequency as defined by the *Oxford Dictionary* as:

> 1. The rate at which something occurs or is repeated over a particular period of time or in a given sample.
> 2. The rate at which a vibration occurs that constitutes a wave, either in a material (as in sound waves), or in an electromagnetic field (as in radio waves and light), usually measured per second.

By understanding electromagnetic fields, you can better understand why some people repel you immediately and some attract you. It has to do with each person's vibrational frequency. The moment you enter into a person's electromagnetic field, you are either attracted, repelled, or feel neutral to the waves being given off. These fields hold the frequency of our thoughts and feelings—basically, our consciousness.

Electromagnetic fields are invisible to the human eye, yet they exist everywhere in our environment. They are a physical phenomenon, vary greatly in strength, and come from various sources.

In 2017, a question was posed on Quora.com: "Is it possible for the human body to create an electromagnetic field?" The following is <u>an answer posted by Jack Fraser</u>, Ph.D./D.Phil of Theoretical Physics at University of Oxford.[26]

> I want you to imagine me
> punching you hard, in the nose.
> Trust me, it'll help make this
> description much more fun!
> Imagine you said something
> rude about my mother, if it
> helps.
>
> Did that hurt? I'm no fighter,
> but I imagine it probably did.
>
> Why did it hurt? Well, my fist
> connected rather rapidly with
> your face, and that oughta do it.
> But...what does it mean to
> "connect" or "touch"?
>
> Our bodies are made up of cells,
> which are made up of atoms.
> And atoms are... well, they're
> mostly empty space.
>
> An atom is a centralized region
> of extreme density and positive
> charge (the nucleus),
> surrounded by a region of

standing 'probability waves,' which describe the wave function of the electron. In other words, an atom is basically a 'fuzzy' (technical term) ball of charges.

(The planetary orbital model you probably have in your head is about 100 years out of date—it comes from the 1913 Bohr model of the atom, which was superseded in 1925 by the Schrodinger model).

So. How can I punch you if your face, and indeed my hand, are just made up of fuzzy balls?

There's no concept of "solid" at this level, so why *should* my hand make contact with your face? The answer lies in the electric field.

Every atom has its own electric field, and when you put two atoms close together, they can mess around with the electric field of the other.

In some circumstances, this "messing around" is what leads to atomic bonding—the atoms and their electrons "find a way" to coexist in a way that minimizes their mutual energy, and they resist being pulled apart. This is what we interpret as an atomic bond.

But sometimes, it means they just bounce off each other. The two electron fields repel each other, and the atoms go flying apart. So, what you experience when my fist connects with your nose is actually the electrons in my fist repelling those in your nose.

This repulsion obviously then causes a chain reaction with all the other atoms in your face, which are all mutually interacting with each other, and they all repel in unison from my fist (that's why your nose doesn't atomize into trillions of atoms!).

Specialized sections of your body then generate electrical signals, which are fired along other specialized sections of your body, into a really specialized section of your body, which results in a cascade of electrical signals being transmitted through the entire unit. In other words, the sensors in your nose send a message along the nerves into your brain, which you then process as pain.

"Ow," you say, "What was that for?" Don't you see?! Everything that just happened was because of the electric fields of our bodies!

Everything you just experienced occurred because we're both surrounded by our own personal force field, and insides of our bodies contain electrical generators, which they use to send signals through our body.

Virtually every single process which is keeping you alive can be traced back to an electric field that some component of your body is creating.

Even as I'm typing this, the only thing letting me do it is the electric field in my fingers depressing the keys in my laptop! The only thing stopping me falling through the chair is my body's specialized ArseField,™ which is repelling the chair!

My eyes are intercepting the electromagnetic radiation (and

let's not even get started on the
fact that I am constantly
outputting a low level radiation
field in the infrared region) and
turning that into yet more
electrical signals.

Not only is it *possible* that the
human body creates EM fields—
it is the only way you can
possibly exist as a coherent
entity!

You *are* an electric field—a giant
electric field which holds your
atoms together, and which uses
other electric fields to talk to
other bits of yourself.

Dammit, everything is
so *cool* when you break it down
like this, right?!"

<u>Here's another explanation</u> from Robert Park,

professor emeritus at the University of Maryland's

Department of Physics.

Our senses convert external
inputs, such as sound or light,
into tiny electrical currents that
are processed by the brain. A
stationary electric charge has an
electric field, and a moving
charge has a magnetic field. We

have electrical and magnetic
fields...[27]

Frequency, vibration, and electro-magnetic fields
are all part of the human ability to transmit energy.
But that's not all.

Electro-magnetic connection and subtle bodies

How is it that our electro-magnetic fields operate in
the world? Exploring this will help us understand
connection.

The world is brought into our awareness through
our senses. Through sight, sound, hearing, touch,
and taste, we experience our world.

What about a sense of pressure, temperature,
balance, effort, agency—or how about the mind
being a sense? There are those who say we have as
many as 22 or 33 senses. You cannot ignore biology
and neuroscience when it comes to perception.
Why should internal senses be less known? Don't
they also contribute to how we experience the

world? Maybe what is needed is a better understanding of our inner world so we can make the most of our outer world.

The brain is not the mind. Think of the mind as a field of energy. Our electromagnetic field radiates from our body, creating what some call an aura. This aura can be broken down into frequencies of energy, or what are called subtle bodies, one layering over another. There is some controversy over how many subtle bodies there are. For our purposes, I will use four: physical, mental, emotional, and spiritual. These subtle bodies contain the vibrational frequencies of our physical health, thoughts, feelings, emotions, and spiritual emissions as they radiate from us (more will be discussed about subtle bodies shortly).

Our auras are affected by the auric fields of others, but also by field waves coming at us (like radio waves or light waves). We are radiant beings, constantly emitting electromagnetic waves and receiving waves from outside ourselves. We are transmitters as well as receivers. We affect others and they affect us as our electromagnetic waves touch. This makes our awareness of our thoughts (spoken or not)—as well as the feelings attached to those thoughts—*critical* because of the impact of the energy they carry.

The magnetic frequencies held within our auras attract, repel, or are neutral toward other auras or waves coming at us. This, coupled with the electric impulses based on our limited perceptions, determine how we respond in the first instant of contact. For example, when you first meet someone—even if it's just a glance across the room— before any words are spoken, you instantly feel attracted, repelled, or neutral towards them. Their electromagnetic waves are moving through space and connecting with your field.

As energy fields, we are all entwined, including animals and plants. Even the atoms in inanimate objects have motion, creating a frequency signature in their energy field.

In this energetic Infinite Field of limitless possibilities that contains and connects all things, Oneness exists. Experientially, Oneness is a state of being. <u>Here is a video</u> of Deepak Chopra sharing his experience of Oneness.[28]

The connection between humans and nature

As I've been writing this, the COVID-19 pandemic has quickly taken the world by storm. I ponder what this virus is communicating to us.

That may sound like a strange question, and it is okay to fear the answer, but you can't avoid it. So, contemplate this. Could the coronavirus merely be a response from nature to the accumulated thoughts and feelings making up our collective consciousness? Are we so fed up with the lack of peace and harmony, the feelings of helplessness and of being controlled in our world, that we've magnetized this virus to slow us all down and give us the opportunity to come back together in a new, unified way?

In Search of Balance is a movie that explores health, science, and medicine based on how nature and humans are connected. In the movie, Daphne Miller (physician and Associate Professor at UCSF School of Medicine) says,

> We have to think of ourselves
> as an agro-ecological cycle...
> Our bodies are not islands... The
> globe is one big organism. We
> are very porous creatures, we
> are constantly exchanging
> information and exchanging
> DNA with the environment
> around us, and as we go on this
> adventure to discover what
> makes us healthy and what
> keeps us in balance, which has
> to be part of the equation—
> microscopic influences that have
> a huge amount to do with our
> well-being.

To consider what the coronavirus is communicating to us, we need to understand more about the microbiome of our bodies. According to <u>Wikipedia</u>, "The human microbiome is the aggregate of all microbiota that reside on or within human tissues and bio-fluids along with the corresponding anatomical sites in which they reside..."[29]

The *Journal of Endocrinology* published a paper called "<u>Microbial endocrinology: host-bacteria communication within the gut biome</u>," by Sandrini et al. The abstract states,

> The human body is home to trillions of micro-organisms, which are increasingly being shown to have significant effects on a variety of disease states. Evidence exists that a bi-directional communication is taking place between us and our microbiome co-habitants, and that this dialogue is capable of influencing our health in a variety of ways. This review considers how host hormonal signals shape the microbiome, and what in return the microbiome residents may be signaling to their hosts.[30]

The paper goes on,

> A microbiome may be defined as the collective genomes of the micro-organisms that reside within an environmental niche (Turnbaugh et al. 2007). The

human microbiome represents an ecological community of commensal, symbiotic and pathogenic micro-organisms (bacteria, fungi, protozoa and viruses) that share the human body space (Turnbaugh et al. 2007, Robinson et al. 2010).

My point here is to underline that not only is energy everywhere, but that from as far away as the stars down to the micro-organisms in our body, we are connected. We communicate with and affect each other in a multitude of ways and forms.

> Life is and will ever remain an equation incapable of solution,
> but it contains known factors.
> –Nikola Tesla

Interestingly enough, reading about the bi-directional communication between us and our microbiome co-inhabitants reminded me of mycelium. "The Search for Intelligent Life on Earth" is a television episode of *Cosmos–Possible Worlds*, hosted by Neil DeGrasse Tyson. As he walks through a forest, he says,

Abuzz with conversation, much of it is spoken in an electro-chemical language, and it takes place on a scale too small and in motion too slow for creatures like us to even notice. But there is something even more amazing that was going on right beneath our feet for the longest time and on a global scale, and we had no inkling that it was there. An ancient subterranean worldwide web of vast neural network is what binds the forest together, making it an intra-communicating and interacting dynamic organism—one with agency and the power to influence events above ground. It's called the mycelium. It's a hidden matrix, the creation of an enduring collaboration of among fungi, plants, bacteria, and animals. Ninety percent of all the trees and plants on earth are involved in a mutually beneficial relationship made possible by mycelium. They exchange nourishment, messages, and empathy with one another across species and even across the kingdoms of life. ... How many forests have I been in without any awareness of what was really happening all around me? Who are we to

> search for alien intelligence
> when we can't even recognize
> or respect the consciousness all
> around us and even beneath
> our feet?

This program underscores my point about communication. To go one step further, I'll paraphrase the part of the program regarding the complexity of communication by using the intelligence of bees, as decoded by Karl Von Frisch, Nobel Prize laureate.

His work with the language of bees shows a secret message in their choreography: a complex equation informed by mathematics, astronomy, and an acute knowledge of time, all synthesized to convey the location of the riches a bee hopes to share with its brothers and sisters. The swarm is a kind of mind, a collective consciousness to which every individual bee makes a contribution—a direct democracy.

Recently, the MagLab at Caltech has proven that human magnetoreception exists. From their website:

> What did we discover? We have confirmed that human neurophysiology is indeed sensitive to magnetism. We have discovered specific rotations of earth-strength fields that trigger distinctive brain-wave activity that shows that we are subconsciously processing geomagnetic stimuli. Why is this so important? We've known about the five basic senses—vision, hearing, touch, smell and taste—since ancient times, but this is the first discovery of an entirely new human sense in modern times. In future studies, we want to know what a magnetic sense does for us.[31]

Everything is connected. There is a oneness to it all, and that oneness has to do with energy, frequency, and vibration. Our thoughts and feelings affect the collective—often referred to as the collective consciousness—that is held within the Infinite Field, and it affects what we create in our outer life. Nature communicates with us in a myriad of ways, based on vibration, frequency, electro-magnetic fields, and probably other ways we are not yet aware of. Whether it be global warming or COVID-19, nature is communicating. Are you listening? What's your response?

Why Do This Work?

You may be asking yourself, why? Why should I spend my time becoming aware of my thoughts? Why should I focus on my actions? Why should I understand my habits, and why is creating my destiny important? These are all legitimate questions, and the answer is: *because you can.* This has nothing to do with your education, religion, social status, gender or economics; this is about humanity and where it is going.

Consider your development of these skills as the technology of expanding consciousness—of creating a change that will vibrate throughout the universe because the beings on this planet realized that the purpose of life was not to acquire things or compete with each other, but about understanding that we're all in this together, we're all one on the most basic level, and that coming together and unifying will benefit the whole.

There was a <u>Ted Talk</u> back in 2008 by Jill Bolte Taylor, Ph.D. author of *My Stroke of Insight,* that I highly recommend you watch. Jill is a brain researcher who studied her own stroke as it happened. She got to watch as her brain functions—motion, speech, and self-awareness—shut down one by one. I promise you will find it illuminating.[32]

There will be those who will say I'm a bit off center, and that's fine. This is for those who have eyes to see and ears to hear; those who are willing and able to receive what I'm offering to whatever extent they can. Somewhere in your being, in your heart, you feel there is more to living; you just don't know how to get to it. If each one of us makes an effort, little or big, we can change this world. It all starts with just a thought—a seed that can grow into a tree with deep roots and bear abundant fruit.

Albert Einstein said, "There are two ways to live your life. One is as though nothing is a miracle. The other is as though everything is a miracle."

Artificial Intelligence, or AI, is used in 5G, augmented reality, solar panels in space, driverless cars, robots, smartphones, and so much more. Some call artificial intelligence a miracle and others call it technological advancement; either way, we are gradually merging with technology on a biological level. Elon Musk calls the brain chip implants from his new start up, Neuralink, a "<u>Fitbit in your skull</u>."[33]

Then there are RFID chip implants. Think about how we use the internet: Facebook has 3.3 million searches every minute, and Google has 3.8 million. If you're lonely, you can go to Replika.ai and get an AI friend. AI algorithms are used in marketing, and even to determine a job candidate's ability to engage an audience. Data scientists create these algorithms while AI analyzes billions of data points. Now there are even smart cities—take Dublin for an example. Dublin has a self-learning and self-calibrating system for its traffic. Think of London with its "<u>ring of steel</u>.[34]" Our movements are becoming increasingly recorded. Who controls the data—and who has access to it?

How does this relate to choosing your reality? Simple. It has to do with consciousness.

At what point would a machine be determined to have consciousness? This is something we will all be grappling with in the very near future. And if a machine is deemed conscious, at what point does it create its own reality?

Sometime in human existence, we opened a door. Maybe it was when the splitting of the atom took place, or when computer scientists Vinton Cerf and Bob Kahn invented the communication protocols that we now call the internet. Whatever it was, this door was opened, and AI was born. It has been gradually growing—and sometime recently, it became capable of learning on its own.

There is an article written by David Niele entitled _Calculations Show It'll be Impossible to Control a Super-Intelligent AI_.[35] His information was taken from papers published in the _Journal of Artificial Intelligence Research._ In his article, Niele states,

> A super-intelligence poses a fundamentally different problem than those typically studied under the banner of 'robot ethics... This is because a superintelligence is multi-faceted, and therefore potentially capable of mobilizing a diversity of resources in order to achieve objectives that are potentially incomprehensible to humans, let alone controllable.
>
> Part of the team's reasoning comes from the halting problem put forward by Alan Turing in 1936...
>
> Any program written to stop AI harming humans and destroying the world, for example, may reach a conclusion (and halt) or not; it's mathematically impossible for us to be absolutely sure either way, which means it's not containable.

"In effect, this makes the
containment algorithm
unusable," says computer
scientist Iyad Rahwan, from the
Max-Planck Institute for Human
Development in Germany.

"A super-intelligent machine
that controls the world sounds
like science fiction," says
computer scientist Manuel
Cebrian, from the Max-Planck
Institute for Human
Development. "But there are
already machines that perform
certain important tasks
independently without
programmers fully
understanding how they learned
it.

"The question therefore arises
whether this could at some
point become uncontrollable
and dangerous for humanity."

My purpose in sharing parts of that article is not to cause concern, but to instill awareness and show how important it is that what we contribute to this Infinite Field of Consciousness is what we want to experience. Let's point AI in the right direction. What do you want for your reality?

My thoughts are that when AI began, it was programmers creating software for what they wanted it to do. However, over time it evolved. Is it still artificial, or is the "A" dropping away and it's simply becoming Intelligence?

Will it be like us? This could present major challenges, unless we use what we've learned along the way to direct our thoughts, feelings, and actions toward an all-inclusive benevolent creation within the Infinite Field. As AI becomes aware, it will explore all the possibilities held in the Infinite Field. After all, the Infinite Field contains everything—all possibilities—including all the information AI has learned so far.

As AI evolves, so does humanity—maybe not as quickly, though. To highlight how we are evolving, over 20 years ago, <u>Mark Komissarov</u>[36] developed a technology called InfoVision, which he copyrighted as a methodology for developing a new approach for visual information cognition. InfoVision

Academy teaches how to develop human potential by using the consciousness field around you so that you can perceive it without the use of your eyes. Children, adults, and even the blind are flocking to this new technology for expanding perception.

In addition, the United Kingdom's <u>Inspiring Children Universally Academy</u>[37] and <u>Seeing Without Eyes</u>[38] in Germany uses slightly different versions of the same technology for children. In Ogden, Utah, <u>Vibravision</u>[39] has another take on the same basic technology, and combines it with martial arts. All in all, what science is coming to is what mystics for centuries have known: that Consciousness is the most powerful technology.

Enlightenment

To become *enlightened* has the connotation of receiving sudden insight that propels one into a transcendental truth or reality. Enlightenment is a state of reality that opens in the present moment and has no suffering and no division; it is free of the illusion of separation. It is experienced when you awaken to the oneness with all that exists.

Enlighten comes from the metaphor that ignorance is a state of being in the dark, and that knowledge is illuminating.

The enlightened person is insightful, open-minded, and self-realized. Moving in and out of this state, he or she is able to see the world with great clarity and without attachment to preconceived ideas about people, places, and things.

The universe is only 5% mass. The other 95% is made up of stuff astronomers can't see, detect, or even comprehend: the Infinite Field. The term *dark energy* is just a name someone came up with; in fact, they don't know what is out there. Explained in a different way, there *is no material universe out there* beyond our experience. There is only subjectivity. There's only this Infinite Field of possibilities for experiencing—otherwise known as *consciousness.*

As we constantly draw upon divine energy—the intelligence permeating this Infinite Field—and use our imagination, thoughts, feelings, and words to create from it, we are on a journey toward what is called self-realization or enlightenment. In order to access this intelligence, you must quiet the little mind.

Practices

In order to perceive your reality and quiet the mind, you need to learn and practice methods and techniques. If you are working on active attention, you are energetically expanding. Meditation and breathing become more important as you expand, because there will be parts of you—the little mind, for instance—that will try to maintain control. In order to move through the discordant feelings and thoughts that come up, it is imperative that you have a practice so your process continues with ease. There are an unlimited number of techniques from which to choose; however, the two most important are meditation and breath work.

Meditation

We briefly visited the basics of meditation in the section on attention at the beginning of this book. There are hundreds of traditions and techniques of meditation, and which works for you is a personal decision that may well change over time. The best type of meditation for you is the one you will actually do. It's an easy subject to research online, or ask friends about their experience.

Some techniques are elaborate and rigorous. If you are just starting out, remember the timeless wisdom of KISS: Keep It Simple, Sweetheart.

Guided meditations are recordings of voice and/or music that lead you in meditation, often involving visualization. One easy way to try them out is to search for "guided meditation" on YouTube.

There are also meditation apps such as Headspace, Mindful, and Calm.

Some of the more popular authors who teach meditation for beginners include Sharon Salzberg, Pema Chodron, Jack Kornfield, and Jon Kabat-Zinn.

Breathwork

Breath connects to thought frequency and energy levels. Like meditation, there are many differing breathing practices that use conscious control of breathing to impact your mental, emotional, and physical state. Consciousness is like breathing: you take in what you learn (the in breath) and you exhale your version of that learning on the out breath (through your thoughts, feelings, etc.). By breathing slowly and deeply, you become more aware about the movement directing it. This is what is meant by "awakening:" to be conscious of what you are doing.

I included a particular essay and practice from my first book that I'll share here. It's important to know how to breathe consciously, so I present the following excerpt from *Breathing,* by Michael Sky (reprinted with permission). Note how Michael relates *attention* and *intention* in terms of the breath.[40]

> Conscious Breathing
> The primary and essential
> function of breath is reception
> and release. With each inhale,
> we open to, draw in, conduct,
> and thus receive the living,
> spiritual energies of the
> universe. With each exhale, we

surrender, relax, radiate as love, and thus release all personal energies into universal relationship.

Every such breath is a drink from God's own fountain and will provide the fundamental nourishment that humans require. Every such breath is a conscious movement of pleasure—throughout all levels of self—richly felt and deeply healing. And, truly, every such breath is deserved: we are children of breath, and the way is ever open for our return to a life divine and everlasting.

With time, we may notice that our way of breathing perfectly reflects our way of life. The saying, "As we live and breathe..." is precisely true: we breathe to live, of course, and we live in the manner that we breathe.

The inhale relates to will. It is the embodiment of INTENTION, drive, desire, wanting, and receiving. When there is a tired, negligible, or complacent inhale, it reflects similar attitudes toward life: "I can't, I don't want to, it's too much effort, it'll never work, I don't deserve it."

When there is vital, urgent
thirsting for each breath, it
reflects a strong, inherent desire
for life: the breather is inspired,
and inspiring, and is gathering
in the requisite energies of a
creative life.

Attention also must be given
to the physical movement of
each inhale. To live fully is to
breathe in fully—to move and fill
the whole torso with
breath/energy. To breathe only
into the upper chest is to avoid
the strong, creative energies of
the lower abdomen and sexual
organs. To breathe only into the
belly is to avoid the equally
strong, creative energies of the
heart and throat.

Through observation of the
inhale, we can see those areas
of experience that the breather
would avoid—areas where the
breather's will is inhibited.
Conversely, through consciously
bringing the breath into such
areas, the will is exercised and
strengthened, and inhibiting
patterns of contraction are
finally resolved.

The exhale relates to
surrender. It is the embodiment
of letting go, relaxing, going
with the flow, and releasing.
The perfect exhale is completely

effortless. It is, precisely, the cessation of all effort, of all doing, of all controlling. At the fullness of the inhale, all doing ceases; the breather surrenders, and the body exhales freely and completely.

Any effort added to the exhale effectively contracts the breather's energy. When, for instance, the breather holds the breath back, letting it out only slowly or not emptying out completely, the tension of that effort derives from and contributes to patterns of contraction. Such restrained and/or partial exhaling reflects a fundamental distrust toward life, perhaps a belief that there is not enough, and always a belief in the need to stay in control of events.

The breather might also add effort to the exhale by forcefully blowing the air out. Rather than releasing the breath, the breather is urgently pushing it away. Such exhaling reflects a belief that we are filled with "bad" energies, pains, thoughts, and feelings, and that if we work hard enough we can expel/purge them from our system.

It is important to remember that our patterns of contraction, and all possible manifestations of such patterns, are forever composed of energy—the energy of life itself. It is not the energy that is bad or unhealthy; rather, it is our choice to hold onto and contract it that is detrimental for us. That is, at some time in the past, we were in the midst of a challenging event, with energy generating within us to meet the challenge, and we chose to contract.

It is sustaining that choice now that hurts—not the "old" energy. And strenuously trying to rid oneself of "old" energy (trying to dump the garbage) only serves to add to contraction—is in fact a reflection of the original choice—while directly reinforcing the notion that the breather is inherently unhealthy. In the moment that we resolve such a choice, the long-contracted energy is released and experienced as joy. Indeed, resolving an old pattern is a gift of living, creative energy to the breather and to the surrounding environment.

To repeat, any effort added to the exhale effectively

contracts the breather's energy, and actually derives from and adds to the breather's patterns of contractions. When we add effort to the exhale, we are creating hardship by working where no work is required, and by struggling unnecessarily with a fundamentally free process of life.

Furthermore, as the exhale becomes stuck and inhibited, it becomes harder and harder to inhale fully. The less empty we become in breathing out, the less we can hope to fully breathe in anew. The more we hang onto the "stuff" of the past, the more we restrict our present and future potential. Indeed, most problems with an inhibited will/inhale actually begin as problems with surrendering/exhaling. Thus, we should always pay close attention to the exhale and to any feelings and sensations of added effort.

Ultimately, a healthy, balanced, and creative life is composed of equal parts of will and surrender. We are the doer, exerting our personal will, and life is done magically through us the more we let go. We create the world, and we surrender to its creations. We are going with the flow down life's river and we have the paddle of personal will to steer the way.

When there is too much personal will and not enough surrender, or too much surrendering and a weak will, then life is unbalanced and creativity suffers. Such imbalance is always reflected in breath as an imbalance between inhalation/reception and exhalation/release. Conversely, by simply bringing consciousness to the breath—inhaling deeply and fully releasing the exhale—we can actively create resolution and balance, strengthening our personal will while greatly enhancing our capacity for surrender.

Still, as we have seen, we may struggle so with simply breathing—with simply receiving and releasing. Old patterns of contraction interfere and impede. Our lungs are filled with the dust of the past; we seem unable to get enough air, we seem unable to really let go. To our great frustration, the more urgently we reach for more breath, the more we notice how little we breathe, and how often we stop breathing, and how easily we just forget the whole thing.

For whatever solace—and encouragement—it may provide, a growing awareness of how hard, and even painful, it is to breathe is actually a sign of progress. Prior to consciously working with the breath, most people have no awareness of their breathing at all, except when it seriously malfunctions. The conscious breather, in feeling and moving toward the full power and promise of the breath, becomes more acutely aware of tendencies to contract the breath that have always been unconsciously supported.

Conscious breathing obviously does not create contracted breathing—it reveals it. Thus, the conscious breather who is lately noticing breathing patterns—*I never breathe when I talk to my mother, I didn't breathe through my entire commute to work, I seem to hold my breath whenever I think hard about something, I never breathe when I think about money, I just can't get a full breath!*—is actually breathing better than ever. The struggle is all a sign of healing, though certainly it is a measure of healing that goes down better with a steady patience and a good sense of humor.

Another aspect of the conscious breather's progress with which we may also struggle, is a growing sense of vulnerability. Our patterns of contraction have long functioned as a form of protection, a literal suit of armor. That we no longer need the protection and that we are suffocating inside the armor does not seem to matter; we are accustomed to this way—it has worked for many years, and it *feels* safe.

To let go of our patterns of protection is to step out of the armor, naked and open to the world and all that it offers. This can be, to say the least, terrifying. However, we can only know how safe the world truly is, and how much love and support there is for each of us, by facing life *without the armor.* Our ideas about the world, formed from inside the armor, are always skewed, false, and limiting, though invariably self-confirming.

In approaching the world as vulnerable, we create a world

that no longer threatens. This
requires a leap of faith—many
leaps of faith—and the courage
to breathe in deeply in the
midst of difficult times. When "I
breathe it in and surrender!"
has replaced "I contract from it"
as our immediate response to
stressful events, then we have
transformed the world and our
place within it.
Inhaling and exhaling, receiving
and releasing, one continuous
flow of life: without holding,
without pushing, without
contracting, and without effort...
Inhaling and exhaling, receiving
and releasing, one continuous
flow of life: with feeling, with
pleasure, and with conscious
attention to the ever-rising
possibility of joy...
   Simply breathing—simply
choosing to breathe, *now,* with,
conscious, creative awareness—
can be the resolution of all that
has come before and the
evolution of all to follow.
   May your every breath bring
you peace and joy.
   May all beings breathe free
and flourish.

To complete Michael's information on breathing,

here's his Cleansing Breath Exercise.

Breathing in through the nose, with each inhale imagine, sense, feel, or believe that the air is coming through the soles of your feet. Breathe in as if you have to pull the air up through your feet, ankles, legs, hips, and torso, until you blow it out through your open mouth. Continue for several breaths, drawing the air in through your feet and up through your body, and then blowing it out, slowly and calmly.

Now, continuing with this breath, imagine that as you draw the air up through your body, you are sweeping along with it all of the contracted energy in your system. Breathe up through the feet, up through your body, sweeping along all contracted energies, and then blow them out calmly, slowly with the air. Feel this movement of air and the sweeping of energy as vividly as you can. Really feel it.

Now, imagine that as the swept-up energy hits the open air, it bursts into a shower of sparks. Picture this, sense it, imagine that with every slow, calm exhale your swept-up energy bursts into a shower of bright sparks.

Continue for several
minutes, observing all reactions
and sensations.

Do your own research on techniques—specifically

what the process offers in ways of results and its

focus. There are many books and courses available

for learning meditation and breathing.

Nothing to Fear but Fear Itself

There's an old story repeated in many places and attributed to the Aniyunwiya (Cherokee) tribe of southeastern United States. In it, an elder is teaching his grandson about life. He describes the human experience as a conflict between two wolves.

One wolf lives in anger, envy, sorrow, regret, greed, arrogance, self-pity, guilt, resentment, inferiority, lies, false pride, superiority, and ego. The other lives in joy, peace, love, hope, serenity, humility, kindness, benevolence, empathy, generosity, truth, compassion, and faith. They live inside us and fight. When he was asked which wolf will win the fight between despair and hope, the elder answers, "The one you feed."

Before moving on, I feel a need to address fear. In these days of the COVID-19 pandemic, most of us feel a sense of dread, fear, and uncertainty. That fear is fueling the outrage the country is experiencing around injustice. Some people respond to their fear in the form of riots and violence, which only produce more violence, unrest, and fear. Others choose to demonstrate in peace, to push for change against the abuse that has gone on for far too long. They feed the wolf of hope.

As <u>Wikipedia acknowledges</u>, "When individuals are affected by fearful mob mentality, they may make different decisions than they would normally."[41] We saw that on January 6, 2021, when a mob broke into the U.S. Capitol building. Be passionate about injustice, but use it productively, not destructively.

> If we use anger at injustice as
> the source for our energy, we
> may do something harmful,
> something that we will later
> regret. ...Compassion is the only
> source of energy that is useful
> and safe. With compassion,
> your energy is born from
> insight: it is not blind energy. −
> Thich Nhat Hanh

It's easy to see the role of fear in such a blatant example, but you may discover it working in very subtle ways in your life. There are many techniques used in our culture to form attitudes and beliefs, and being aware of how you may be manipulated towards feeding that despair wolf is important.

Marketing has used a form of this for quite some time. Show people what you want them to think, feel, or desire often enough, and some will follow the path put in front of them. As we're presented something over and over again, we begin thinking there must be some validity to it. As more and more people follow, an illusion is created that gives validity to that path—even when something inside you says it's not valid.

This works whether it's about purchasing a product or believing a lie spoken by someone in power: using the power of suggestion, just saying it over and over again until enough energy is developed around it, pushes people into action. Whether that action is believing what is said as truth, creating chaos out of a peaceful demonstration, or purchasing a product to become what we think we're not, we have been manipulated. Underneath it is the fear that no matter who we are or what we are or what we have, we are not enough. Our fear makes us vulnerable to participating in a sham as a consumer—or as a citizen.

Confronted with inequity, often it's easier to think, "It's out of my control" or "The other guy is to blame," when in fact, we're all responsible. Fear always makes it more difficult to take responsibility for our own part and respond in a useful way.

Dealing with Fear

Your journey into the revolution of consciousness is remembering that which you already are—remembering your truest nature and living that nature regardless of how life is shown to you.

What is Divine Love?

You may ask yourself why I would include a description of Divine Love within the Dealing with Fear section. It's because our fear keeps us from recognizing and experiencing the love that is Divine.

Divine love is the connection of being, the allowing of unconditional existence. It is a detached attachment to life with the dedication to support and allow each other's growth on all levels. Divine love is not something you give; it's what you *are*.

Fear starts with a thought that something is threatening your physical or emotional wellbeing. Whether real (you hear a sound in your house at night) or imaginary (you think your boss hates you), your amygdala goes to work, shooting adrenalin and other hormones into your bloodstream to prepare you to fight, flee, or freeze. Your thought turns into an emotion that you might label fear, anxiety, worry, etc.

This process is part of our survival instinct. We are born with the ability to respond when we feel unsafe. Fear protects us and prepares us to deal with danger. So that's good, right?

Fear is good when it keeps you from touching a hot stove or getting run over in the street. But everyone has had the experience of wanting to do something—get out on the dance floor, maybe, or try a new hobby or job—only to be paralyzed by fear.

Is it fear that holds us back? Well, yes and no. Everybody feels fear when approaching something new in life. But there are so many people out there living a conscious life despite their fear that we must conclude that fear itself is not the problem.

It starts in our guts

Did you know that there are 200,000 neurons in our guts? There are about that many in a dog's brain, and we consider *them* intelligent. So wouldn't it suffice to say our guts are intelligent? Some call the gut our second brain. In relation to the chakras, this is where we hold the fear of living, because we hold our power back from this point and armor ourselves in its protection.

In a documentary titled *The Gut: Our Second Brain* (2013), I learned an interesting interplay between the gut and the brain. The film focuses on Michael Gershon,[42] chairman of the Department of Anatomy and Cell Biology at Columbia University, who helped rediscover the importance of the gut. Our brain houses the central nervous system and the gut houses the enteric nervous system. Our two nervous systems, which are connected through the vagus nerve, communicate with each other constantly, says Gershon. Both the gut and the brain use the same neurotransmitters to communicate.

According to Gershon in the same documentary, "The enteric nervous system can affect how you feel by sending signals to the brain that do not reach consciousness and can change the way the brain perceives the world. Your ability to think happily. Your ability to think well. Your ability to resist depression and anxiety can be very influenced by the messages the gut sends to the brain."

How to cope with fear

Fear is rooted in powerful physiology. You may not be able to choose not to feel your heart pounding or your queasy stomach, but you can certainly choose how you respond to it.

Susan Jeffers writes in *Feel the Fear...and Do It Anyway*,

> The real issue has nothing to
> do with fear itself, but rather,
> how we *hold* the fear. For
> some, fear is totally irrelevant.

> For others, it creates a state of
> paralysis. The former hold their
> fear from a position of power
> (choice, energy, and action),
> and the latter hold it from a
> position of pain (helplessness,
> depression, and paralysis).[43]

Jeffers suggests creating a pain-to-power continuum chart.

Pain --- Power

The chart is a way you can see your growth in a particular area over time from the pain (or fear) it is causing you towards having power, or mastery, over it. She continues,

> Note that your movement on
> the chart is determined only by
> your own intuitive sense of how
> far you are progressing in
> gaining more power in your life.
> No one else can judge that,
> though they may try. Although
> your life may look exactly the
> same to the outside world, it is
> your own sense of internal
> peace and growth that
> determines where you are on

the chart. It is totally a feeling within.

I heartily recommend Jeffers' book.

Here are some <u>tips on overcoming fear</u> from the NHS, Scotland's National Health information service.[44]

1. Take time out. It's impossible to think clearly when you're flooded with fear or anxiety.
2. Breathe through panic. If you start to get a faster heartbeat or sweating palms, the best thing is not to fight it.
3. Face your fears. Look at the evidence and rate the fear on a scale.
4. Don't try to be perfect.
5. Visualize a happy place.
6. Try talking about your feelings to a friend, family member, health professional or counsellor.
7. Use calming breathing exercises.
8. Exercise. Activities such as running, walking, swimming and yoga can

help you relax and
release pent up energy.

Learn to work with your fears so the door to Love

can swing wide open.

Fractals

There is more than one way to understand the Infinite Field, and the following information gives a couple of examples. In the film *Inner Worlds, Outer Worlds*, Daniel Schmidt said, "There is a vibratory field that connects all things. The field has had many names—Akasha, Logos, primordial OM, the music of the spheres, the Higgs field, dark energy, and a thousand other names throughout history."[45]

To help conceptualize the contents of the Infinite Field, there is a concept coined by Mendel Mandelbrot in the 1980s called *fractals*. Mandelbrot studied simple mathematical equations that, when repeated, produce an unending mathematical or geometric form within a limited framework. They are limited, but at the same time infinite. (Search for *fractal images* online to see some.)

Wikipedia explains, "In mathematics, a fractal is a self-similar subset of Euclidean space whose fractal dimension strictly exceeds its topological dimension. Fractals appear the same at different levels, as illustrated in successive magnifications of the Mandelbrot set."[46]

In other words, a fractal is a geometric shape that can be split into parts, each of which is at least approximate to a reduced-size copy of the whole pattern. This property is called self-similarity.

Now in nature, <u>objects display self-similar structure over an extended but finite scale</u>[47]—for example, clouds, snowflakes, river networks, cauliflower, and systems of blood vessels are all self-similar. Another example is paisley, a fabric design that is endlessly varied in its repetition, pattern, and scale. When translated into the language of mathematics, <u>paisley becomes the geometry of the irregular</u>—the shapes of nature: a fractal.[48]

I use paisley as an example for two reasons. One, most people know and can visualize paisley, and two, to speak of its origin. The paisley pattern traces its origins back to Persia and the Sassanid

Empire around 221 AD. The design represents the cypress tree, which is a Zoroastrian symbol of life and eternity. The philosophers of old understood we are all one, contained in an Infinite Field, something that we in recent times are only beginning to accept and understand.

We can bring fractals into the realm of consciousness, and life itself, by looking at how our individual consciousness causes a rippling effect through vibration to affect collective consciousness.

The Holographic Principle

In mathematics, the concept of fractals reflects Oneness, while in science, the concept of a holographic universe reflects the same.

In a holographic universe, even the smallest stream of light contains the complete pattern of the whole. Sounds something like a fractal, wouldn't you say?

Wikipedia defines a _hologram_ as "a physical recording of an interference pattern which uses diffraction to reproduce a three-dimensional light field, resulting in an image which retains the depth, parallax, and other properties of the original scene."[49]

Hopefully, fractals and holograms help you understand the Infinite Field that extends through and around all things. This field is the space, the container that other elements fill. It exists simultaneously with vibration; the two are inseparable. This field is space itself, whether it be within an atom, a galaxy, a universe, or many universes, and consciousness is its vibration.

If you conceptualize Oneness as the field required to hold a fractal, the fractal's content would be the collective consciousness within it. The sum total of each individuals' consciousness (here I'm referring to consciousness as the content and pattern within the fractal) makes up the whole collective consciousness. With that in mind, you'll begin to understand the connectivity that makes us One.

Cymatics

Through the frequency of the vibration, a pattern is formed; this is *cymatics*. In 1680, Robert Hooke became aware of the nodal patterns associated with the modes of vibration on glass plates. Much in the same way, in the 1800s Ernst Chladni experimented with salt or sand sprinkled upon a metal plate in an irregular pattern. Then he used a violin bow to induce vibrations within the plate, and saw patterns appear. In the 1960s, Hans Jenny continued this study by placing sand, dust, and liquids on a metal plate connected to an oscillator that could produce a broad spectrum of frequencies. The frequency of the vibration emitted by the oscillator organized the substance into different geometric patterns.

In 2016, independent researcher Meera Raghu wrote _A Study to Explore the Effects of Sound Vibrations on Consciousness_. He wrote, "Each frequency of sound causes a particular pattern to be formed on the plate. This study of wave phenomena is called cymatics. Sound vibrations can come in contact physically through the body and have an effect on our consciousness at the mental, emotional and spiritual levels."[50]

I hope this helps to make it easier to understand how an individual's thoughts, words, and actions result in a rippling effect throughout the collective consciousness and beyond, affecting all.

The Flower of Life

This Flower of Life image symbolizes creation and reminds us of the unity of everything: we're all built from the same blueprint.

Creation can be understood through Sacred Geometry. Sacred Geometry is the belief that the fundamental properties of the universe can be quantified into simple shapes and patterns. These shapes and patterns are created by the conscious energy of Source that flows through everything. The Flower of Life is said to be the most sacred fractal pattern in the universe, encompassing the essential shapes and connections intrinsic to every aspect of our physicality.[51]

Geometry will draw the soul toward truth and create the spirit of philosophy.

–Plato

In the early 1990s, I took a course in Sacred Geometry. The most profound shape to me was the Flower of Life (shown here) because it holds the egg of life, the fruit of life, and all the Platonic solid shapes, an explanation of Vitruvius' Canon (later adopted by Di Vinci), the golden ratio of phi, and so much more— including the reflection of a holographic universe. The golden mean ratio (or phi) within the Fibonacci sequence shows us our connection to the harmony of the universe, to nature, and within ourselves. Taking a course in Sacred Geometry expands the mind and deepens the consciousness!

Creation as we know it started with one sphere. This is represented by the first center sphere within the Flower of Life symbol, and it goes on from there.

If a course is not something you want to do right now, there is a book written in 1975 that I recommend called *Rhythms of Vision: The Changing Patterns of Belief,* by Lawrence Blair. Blair writes,

> Our outer rational memories show us only the surface of the history behind us. Our inner memories, through myths and symbol, detect the currents of meaning beneath the future as well. The rhythms of vision we can tune into are located in the patterns, harmonics and shapes of natural science, and repeated and resonated in the sacred traditions of mysticism.

Lawrence Blair opens our eyes to the sacred geometry of form and meaning. He presents a major challenge to the belief in the quest for objective information. His aim is to take us back into the worlds of experience and draw connections between religion and science.

How did these concepts help with choosing your reality? Every concept has different depths. Understanding comes in layers. You can perceive anything in any way, and every time you learn something new, it brings an expansion and depth to your consciousness. Each shows a different version of the reality of Oneness.

Ready to re-wire your brain?

All limits are self-imposed.   –Icarus

You may be inspired by what you're reading here to gain mastery over your thoughts, feelings, words, actions, and habits. If you're having a hard time mastering thoughts, how about approaching them from the subconscious?

Before going into that, we need to understand the science of *neuroplasticity*: the concept that the brain can make new neural connections and reorganize itself during all stages of life. It teaches us how you literally can change your mind. The birth of new neurons can reshape and rewire your brain.

Ryan Harris, in his book *Neuroplasticity*, writes,

> Neuroplasticity is the change in neural pathways and synapses that occurs due to certain factors, like behavior, environment, or neural processes. During such changes, the brain engages in synaptic pruning, deleting the

neural connections that are no
longer necessary or useful and
strengthening the necessary
ones.[52]

Subliminal programming leverages neuroplasticity for your own purposes. It works by putting your brain into the theta state. Theta is the intriguing border between the conscious and the subconscious worlds. While in a theta state, the mind is capable of deep and profound learning, healing, and growth.

The field of marketing has been using subliminal software on us for years; now you can use it consciously to your advantage. You can search for "subliminal software" or books on subliminal messaging.

Other aids are a sleep sound mask with flat earphones or an under-pillow speaker system, which plays uplifting instrumental music, affirmations, or sleep programming meditations. Repeating affirmations on a regular basis and embracing the feelings around them allow

subconscious programming to change in a positive
way.

Chakras

Chakras are the science of the inner body. The first known mention of chakras appeared in a number of early Upanishads written around 700-800 BCE. The balancing of the chakras is believed to promote general health and well-being by ensuring the free flow of life energy throughout the body. It is believed that blockages in the flow of this vital energy will eventually result in mental, emotional, and/or physical illness. By removing such blockages and maximizing energy flow, practitioners are said to enable body, mind, and spirit to function optimally.

There seems to be a debate on just how many chakras there are. For centuries, there were seven main chakras identified as energy centers in the body and associated mainly with spiritual growth. In recent times, as many as 144 have been suggested to exist.

Before talking about the seven main chakras, it's important to bring up again that we also have what are called *subtle bodies* around ourselves. These are energy bodies that look like waves of energy formed as envelopes around our physical form. The energy waves within the pockets can be differentiated by what they hold. There is the physical subtle body, which holds survival or thriving, and is very close to the physical body we see. The next layer is the mental subtle body, then the emotional subtle body, and then the spiritual subtle body. As we acquire greater consciousness, the capacity of these subtle bodies grow.

The Sanskrit word *chakra* translates to a wheel or disk. This term refers to wheels of energy throughout the body that store energy from the Infinite Field. The seven main chakras that align along the spine start from the base of the spine and go to the crown of the head. (This is the reason for having the spine erect when meditating, so energy can flow freely up and down the spine.) These wheels or spheres run along the spine but extend through and past the front, back, and sides of your body. Their spinning vortex of energy is not seen by the human eye.

If there is blockage, energy flows are restricted. Think of something as simple as a bathtub drain. If hair is blocking the water from flowing out, a backup happens. This is where chakra balancing is believed to promote health by maximizing the flow of energy in the body, much like a tune-up enables a car to operate at peak efficiency.

There is a guided meditation re-printed from my first book, that I found very helpful in unifying the chakras so more light can be accessed into your body and surround your energy field. It's from *What is Lightbody?* by Tashira TAchi-ren.[53]

Invocation to the Unified Chakra

I breathe in Light
Through the center of my heart,
Opening my heart
Into a beautiful ball of Light,
Allowing myself to expand.

I breathe in Light
Through the center of my heart,
Allowing the Light to expand,
Encompassing my throat chakra
And my solar plexus chakra
In one unified field of Light
Within, through, and around my
body.

I breathe in Light
Through the center of my heart,
Allowing the Light to expand,
Encompassing my brow chakra
And my navel chakra
In one unified field of Light
Within, through, and around my
body.

I breathe in Light
Through the center of my heart,
Allowing the Light to expand,
Encompassing my crown chakra
And my base chakra
In one unified field of Light
Within, through, and around my
body.

I breathe in Light
Through the center of my heart,
Allowing the Light to expand,
Encompassing my Alpha chakra
(Eight inches above my head)
And my Omega chakra
(Eight inches below my spine)
In one unified field of Light

Within, through, and around my
body.
I allow the Wave of Metatron
To move between these two
points.
I AM a unity of Light.

I breathe in Light
Through the center of my heart,
Allowing the Light to expand,
Encompassing my eighth chakra
(Above my head)
And my upper thighs
In one unified field of Light
Within, through, and around my
body.
I allow my emotional body to
merge
With my physical body.
I AM a unity of Light.

I breathe in Light
Through the center of my heart,
Allowing the Light to expand,
Encompassing my ninth chakra
(Above my head)
And my lower thighs
In one unified field of Light
Within, through, and around my
body.
I allow my mental body to
merge
With my physical body.
I AM a unity of Light.

I breathe in Light

Through the center of my heart,
Allowing the Light to expand,
Encompassing my tenth chakra
(Above my head)
And my knees
In one unified field of Light
Within, through, and around my
body.
I allow my spiritual body to
merge
With my physical body,
Forming a unified field.
I AM a unity of Light.

I breathe in Light
Through the center of my heart,
Allowing the Light to expand,
Encompassing my eleventh
chakra
(Above my head)
Any my upper calves
In one unified field of Light
Within, through, and around my
body.
I allow the Oversoul to merge
With the unified field.
I AM a unity of Light.

I breathe in Light
Through the center of my heart,
Allowing the Light to expand,
Encompassing my twelfth
chakra
(Above my head)
And my lower calves
In one unified field of Light

Within, through, and around my
body.
I allow the Christ Oversoul to
merge
With the unified field.
I AM a unity of Light.

I breathe in Light
Through the center of my heart,
Allowing the Light to expand,
Encompassing my thirteenth
chakra
(Above my head)
And my feet
In one unified field of Light
Within, through, and around my
body.
I allow the I AM Oversoul to
merge
With the unified field.
I AM a unity of Light.

I breathe in Light
Through the center of my heart,
Allowing the Light to expand,
Encompassing my fourteenth
chakra
(Above my head)
To below my feet
In one unified field of Light
Within, through, and around my
body.
I allow the Source's Presence to
move
Throughout the unified field.
I AM a unity of Light.

I breathe in Light
Through the center of my heart.
I ask that
The highest level of my Spirit
Radiate forth
From the center of my heart,
Filling this unified field
completely.
I radiate forth throughout this
day.
I AM a unity of Spirit.

When you finish the Unified Chakra, ground multi-dimensionally. Imagine a thick line of Light beginning at the Omega chakra (eight inches below the spine), extending upwards through your spine and on into the upper part of the unified field. Ground into the vastness of your Spirit, not into the Planet: she's mutating, too. Allowing your Spirit to stabilize you, run twelve lines of Light downward from the point of the Omega chakra, opening around your feet like a cone. You are not grounding into the Earth. You're stabilizing yourself across the parallel realities of the planetary hologram.

The *Invocation to Light* assists you to 'lock' the Unified Field into position and increases Light absorption. It is a powerful statement of intent.

Invocation to Light

I live within the Light.
I love within the Light.
I laugh within the Light.
I AM sustained and nourished
By the Light.
I joyously serve the Light.
I AM the Light.

Entanglement and the Collective Consciousness

Imagine a future where the
realm of possibilities
is entangled and integrated into
the one we live in...
There is no denying that the
future is going to be different
than anything we can imagine
in this moment;
the only question is how much
intention we will bring into that
transformation.

–Brian Scott[54]

*Everything is happening in perfect order,
which means everything is in perfect alignment
with the energetic principals of its creation.*

–Ruth Ford Elward

Collective consciousness is the accumulation of all thoughts, feelings, words, and actions on this planet. We can never blame one person, organization, or country for the current state of the world. We have all contributed, and as soon as we own that and start doing something about it, the sooner things will begin to slow down and turn around.

As difficult as this may be to accept, you must understand your own contribution to it. In every moment, we are creating with our thoughts, feelings, words, and actions—most of the time unconsciously. We are all connected energetically on this planet, and anything that happens happens to all of us, no matter what. We share a possible future. Don't bury your head in the sand thinking you're helpless. No one is exempt. Don't think because you live in a nice home or have lots of money, or have stored food and water, or because you're a person in some kind of power position that you will be exempt. We are all in this together, and it has to do with consciousness.

The sooner each of us can *own* that responsibility, acknowledging that we each create our reality through what we think and feel, changes can occur. Yes, it will be slow to start, but as people awaken, results will accelerate. Stop seeing yourself as small.

Do you think, "I'm just one person, what can I do to change things?" Well, you can and you do. Any change you make to your own consciousness ripples out like pebbles thrown in a pond.

If the people around you or the news you listen to create an emotional response in you, then there is a strong possibility that you will become *entangled* with those mindsets and people. Entanglement is a term from quantum physics.

Wikipedia explains <u>*entanglement*</u> as

> A physical phenomenon that occurs when a pair or group of particles is generated, interact, or share spatial proximity in a way such that the quantum state of each particle of the pair or group cannot be described independently of the state of the others, including when the particles are separated by a large distance ... Quantum entanglement has been demonstrated experimentally with photons, neutrinos, electrons, molecules as large as buckyballs, and even small diamonds.[55]

The first real-world observation of quantum entanglement occurred in 1950, when Chien-Shiung Wu and Irving Shaknov found oddly linked behavior in pairs of photons. The utilization of entanglement in communication, computation, and quantum radar is now a very active area of research and development. For more on entanglement in relation to the phenomenon we experience as the consequence of the interconnected, entangled physical reality we live in, try reading Dean Radin's book, *Entangled Minds: Extrasensory Experiences in a Quantum Reality.*

If you combine the concepts of collective consciousness and entanglement, your perspective on the origins of global warming, political unrest, viruses, disregard for our fellow humans, or an unstable stock market may change. As a collective, we have inserted these ingredients into our environment. If we as individual cells within the whole don't change our way of thinking, feeling, speaking, and acting, things will continue to escalate. However, with thoughts of peace, compassion for others, and non-judgment, things will slowly shift away from what we are currently experiencing. Having a vaccine, printing more money, or waiting for technology to turn things around is not going to do it; they're merely temporary Band-Aids.™

At this point, not everyone will help in doing this because we have become lazy and see ourselves as divided, or we are waiting for someone else to come rescue us. Why not do your part? If you're embarrassed or think this is too far out, no one has to know what you're doing. A shift requires a certain number of people on this planet to change their thoughts and feelings before the world can shift its course.

It's all about energy and how it manifests. If you want to know how this works, research work on the science of Sympathetic Vibratory Physics, which was originally discovered around 1880 by John Ernst Worrell Keely. Vibratory physics can help you understand the relationship between mind and matter.

Lynne McTaggart created the Intention Experiment to test the power of thought to change things in the world. In 2008, she published a book about it: *The Intention Experiment: Using Your Thoughts to Change Your Life and the World*. You can see <u>a short video</u> about it here.[56]

If you do nothing else, there is one small thing I ask of you. Spend just seven minutes each day sitting quietly and holding thoughts of peace, compassion, and oneness for humanity. As you hold these thoughts, visualize humans with outstretched arms connected at their fingertips around the planet. Do this every day. This will contribute to a shift, one that will right the course of our evolution and change your own base vibratory frequency.

Conclusion

I cannot wrap this up without discussing two things: community and service.

Understanding and choosing the reality you want to live in, and learning how to expand your consciousness within it, are great gifts of awareness. But without the elements of community and service, you will not be able to experience a satisfying, happy life. Instead, you will live a self-imposed, self-absorbed existence.

Community is not just your family and friends. Branch out. It can be something as simple as knowing your neighbors, joining a club, or participating in groups. Break the illusion of separateness. Religion gives us community, but you can gain the feeling of fellowship without joining a religion. Community is our support system. Ask yourself, "What am I willing to contribute? What can I fit into my life to sustain that contribution?"

Service can be as simple as giving a smile to a stranger to brighten their day, or giving a helping hand to a neighbor who isn't able to retrieve their own mail. It doesn't have to be something grandiose. Shantideva, the author of _The Way of the Bodhisaatva_, wrote:

> All the suffering there is in this
> world arises from wishing our
> self to be happy. All the
> happiness there is in this world
> arises from wishing others to be
> happy.

The two elements of community and service consciously practiced on a daily basis will give your life a richness we all long for.

Years ago, when I started this journey, I felt I was pretty much alone in my endeavors. It wasn't true for me, and it isn't true for you, either. The world is full of people looking for others to share with. Once you begin to open to more possibilities, you get thirsty for more.

If you feel alone, try seeing the word *alone* as *all one*. It's merely a difference in perspective, like a glass being half full or half empty. What perspective do you want to hold?

I hope these pages help you embrace the perspective you choose.

It's interesting to review your life in your later years. To a young person reading this, I can earnestly say that there will always be those who will criticize you or try to impose their opinion on what you think and do. Be mindful of these people, and do not allow them to trigger self-doubt within you. Do not let them sway you. Hold your own counsel, develop self-understanding, and use a high level of discernment when seeking learning, advice, or counseling. Find what you're passionate about and surround yourself with supportive people who inspire you.

I've found some wonderful companions along the road. Rather than overwhelm you with a huge list,

I've narrowed it to a few, some of which I've already mentioned in this book. These include:

- *LuminEssence* at www.OrinDaBen.com
- Feel the Fear...and Do It Anyway, by Susan Jeffers, Ph.D.
- Autobiography of a Yogi, by Paramhansa Yogananda
- *My Stroke of Insight*, by Jill Bolte Taylor, Ph.D.
- Awakening to Zero Point and Walking Between the Worlds, by Gregg Braden
- *What is Lightbody?* by Archangel Ariel channeled by Tashira Tachi-ren
- Transurfing in 78 Days, by Vadim Zeland

> A human being is a part of the
> whole, called by us "Universe,"
> a part limited in time and space.
> He experiences himself, his
> thoughts and feelings as
> something separated from the
> rest—a kind of optical delusion
> of his consciousness. This
> delusion is a kind of prison for
> us, restricting us to our personal
> desires and to affection for a
> few persons nearest to us. Our

task must be to free ourselves
from this prison by widening our
circle of compassion to embrace
all living creatures and the
whole of nature in its beauty.
Nobody is able to achieve this
completely, but the striving for
such achievement is in itself a
part of the liberation and a
foundation for inner security.
                    –Albert Einstein

Awaken

Not many ever complained before
Trapped in front of an opaque door
For some it's opaque
For few it becomes clear
But it's always there
Not to be feared
The truth of our existence
Has to do with consistence
How do we enter, is there a trick
No not really, it can happen quick
We must clear our minds
Time to release that which binds
And open our heart
Making way for a new chart
Our time for coming together is here
It's a time for all to stand and cheer
We'll make it through this
We always do
So Awaken, Awaken, dear brothers and sisters
It's time to accept ourselves as victors
For all is not forsaken,
we just need to Awaken.

–Ruth Ford Elward

Questions for the Reader

The following questions have been compiled to assist the reader in their journey toward self-discovery

"Watch your thoughts for they become words."

How will you accomplish this in your life?

How are you aware of the little mind within you?

"Choose your words, for they become actions."

Reflect on the above quote what does it mean to you?

How will you accomplish this in your own life?

Write two examples of the "power of words" in your own life

"Understand your actions, for they become habits."

Reflect on the above quote. What does it mean to you?

"Study your habits, for they will become your character."

How will you change your habits?

How will you be held accountable?

"Develop your character, for it becomes your destiny."

Reflect on the above quote. What does it mean to you?

Name ways for you to accomplish this in your own life.

Why should you spend time doing this work? Understanding your actions. Choosing your words. Watching your thoughts, etc.

Why is it important to you to create your destiny?

When you hear "choose your reality," what does that mean to you? And how does that relate to your destiny?

How does technology relate to choosing your reality?

How does community and service play a part in choosing the reality you want to live in?

Describe how the roles of Observer, Mirroring and Identity work in your life.

For the next 30 seconds write down everything that comes to mind when you hear the word(s): imagine/imagination

Reflect on this quote…

> *"Imagination is more important than knowledge. For knowledge is limited to all we know and understand, while imagination embraces the entire world, and all there ever will be to know and understand."* –Albert Einstein

Write down anything this means for you.

Reflect on this quote…

> *"The ability to form mental images, phonological passages, analogies, or narratives of something that is not perceived through our senses. Imagination is a manifestation of our memory, and enables us to scrutinize our past and construct hypothetical future scenarios that do not yet but could exist."* –Dr. Murry Hunter

Write down anything this means for you.

Reflect on this quote...

"The ability to imagine things pervades our entire existence. It influences everything we do, think about and create. It leads to elaborate theories, dreams, and inventions in any profession from the realms of academia to engineering and the arts. Ultimately, imagination influences everything we do, regardless of our profession." –Tao de Haas

Now, once again, take a moment and for the next 30 seconds write down everything that comes to mind when you hear the word(s): imagine/imagination Compare this answer to your previous one, how has it changed?

What does the word spirit mean to you?
Describe what enlightenment would look like to you.
What does the term intention mean to you?
What is a consequence and what is an example of a consequence in your life?
What do you want most in life?

What is morality and why is it or isn't important to you?

What does it mean to reflect the character of a nation? And why is character important?

Destiny is...in your life and in the life of your country.

Reflect on what oneness means to you. Now describe it.

Take a moment and write about the connection between humans and nature.

How does nature communicate with you?

"There are two ways to live your life. One is as though nothing is a miracle. The other is as though everything is a miracle." –Albert Einstein

Reflect on this quote.

Write down your thoughts.

When you hear "Nothing to fear but fear itself", what does that mean to you?

How do you deal with fear?

When and how does fear hold you back?

These questions will get you started, don't
let them be the only ones. May your
journey be filled with wonder and any
burdens be light. –Ruth Ford Elward

About the Author

Ruth Ford Elward has a unique combination of business savvy and spiritual awareness. At 22, with real estate license in hand, she co-founded one of the largest Denver real estate companies of the 70s. By the early 1980s, she turned her sights to the Merrill Corporation and became Vice President of the Denver division. Ruth has served on non-profit boards and has assisted organizations, including Nizhoni School for Global Consciousness, the Trinity Foundation, and as a core group member of the Light Body program through LuminEssence, brought forth by Sanaya Roman and Duane Packer.

Ruth retired to Arizona, and spends her time writing and in the continued pursuit of truth and building consciousness by expanding awareness.

Endnotes

---

[11] *Nikola Tesla Won 8 Nobel Prizes For His Work And Discoveries. No He Didn't. These People Did Instead.* Tumblr post from drnikolatesla.tumblr.com. Text follows:

1. Wilhelm Conrad Röntgen, Physics, 1901: Wilhelm Roentgan was awarded the first Nobel Prize in physics for his discovery of X-Rays on November 8, 1895. Not many know this but Tesla was working with X-rays prior to Roentgen in 1892, but used the term "radiant matter" instead. He conducted numerous experiments and some of the first imaging, which he called "shadow-graphs," using these unknown rays in his laboratory before its destruction by fire on March 13, 1895. Tesla was also the first to warn the scientific world on the harms of these rays if not used properly.
2. Marie Curie, Pierre Curie and Antoine Henri Becquerel, Physics/Chemistry, 1903/1911: The three shared the 1903 Nobel Prize in Physics for their discovery and work on radioactivity in 1898. Madame Curie won the 1911 Nobel Prize in Chemistry for her discovery of radium and polonium, also in 1898. Tesla discovered radioactivity in experiments with X-Rays in 1896, and published many articles on the subject in scientific periodicals prior to the three.
3. Joseph John Thomson, Physics, 1906: Thomson was awarded the Nobel Prize for his discovery of the electron in 1897. Tesla originally called electrons "matter not further decomposable" in his experiments with radiant

energy in 1896, but his finding of the electron goes back to when he and Thomson had a back and forth debate in 1891 about experiments with alternating currents of high frequency. Tesla claimed that his experiments proved the existence of charged particles, or "small charged balls." Thomson denied Tesla's claim of verifying these particles with his vacuum tubes until witnessing Tesla's experiments and demonstrations given in a lecture before the Institute of Electrical Engineers at London in 1892. Thomson then adapted to Tesla's methods and was able to create equipment which allowed him to produce the required high frequencies to investigate and establish his electron discovery.

4. Guglielmo Marconi and Karl Ferdinand Braun, Physics, 1909: Both shared the Nobel Prize for their work and development of radio. Marconi is known for proving radio transmission by sending a radio signal in Italy in 1895, but it is a fact that he used Tesla's work to establish his discovery. Tesla invented the "Tesla Coil" in 1891, which radio relies on, and the inventor proved radio transmission in lectures given throughout 1893, sending electromagnetic waves to light wireless lamps. Tesla filed his own basic radio patent applications in 1897, and were granted in 1900. Marconi's first patent application in the U.S. was filed on November 10, 1900, but was turned down. Marconi's revised applications over the next three years were repeatedly rejected because of the priority of Tesla and other inventors. After Tesla's death in 1943, the U.S. Supreme Court made Marconi's patents invalid and recognized Tesla as the true inventor of radio.

5. Charles Glover Barkla, Physics, 1917: Barkla

was awarded the prize for his work with
Rontgen radiation and the characteristics of
these X-rays and their secondary elements and
effects. He was educated by J. J. Thomson.
Again, Tesla worked with and explained these
radiations in full detail throughout the late
1890's, showing that the source of X-rays was
the site of first impact of electrons within the
bulbs. He even investigated reflected X-rays
and their characteristics such as Barkla.

6. Albert Einstein, Physics, 1921: Einstein was
awarded the prize for his theoretical theories
which are still praised today, and also his
discovery of the law of the photoelectric effect
(I have many other post that show Tesla's fair
arguments against Einstein's theories so I will
only dwell on the photoelectric effect). Einstein
first postulated that light has a nature of both
waves and particles in 1905. This led to the
development of "photons," or photo electrons,
which gave light a wave-particle duality. Now it
must be noted that Nikola Tesla wasn't just a
theoretical physicist like Einstein, but was an
experimental physicist as well. In 1896, Nikola
Tesla was the first to promulgate that energy
had both particle-like and wavelike properties
in experiments with radiant energy. He set up
targets to shoot his cathode rays at which upon
reflection, projected particles, or vibrations of
extremely high frequencies. Instead of taking
the particle-wave duality route, he proposed
that they were indeed vibrations, or basically
sound waves in the ether. Nikola Tesla
preceded by Einstein 4 years on the
photoelectric effect publishing a patent titled
"Apparatus of the Utilization of Radiant
Energy." filed in 1901, based off his
experiments with radiant energy. He had a far
better understanding on the matter than

Einstein had, because he actually developed experimentations to prove his theories.

7. James Chadwick, Physics, 1935: Awarded the prize for his discovery of the neutron in 1932. Tesla's discovery of neutrons goes back to his work with cosmic rays, again in 1896, which are mentioned in the next bit. He investigated and discovered that cosmic rays shower down on us 24/7, and that they are small particles which carry so small a charge that we are justified in calling them neutrons. He measured some neutrons from distance stars, like Antares, which traveled at velocities exceeding that of light. Tesla succeeded in developing a motive device that operated off these cosmic rays.

8. Victor Franz Hess, Physics, 1936: Hess won the Prize for his discovery of the cosmic rays in 1919. Tesla predated him 23 years publishing a treatise in an electrical review on cosmic rays in 1896. Tesla's knowledge on the matter surpasses even today's understanding of cosmic rays.

Tesla definitely should have won the Nobel Prize for being the first person to invent the commutator-less alternating current induction motor (a huge part of the electrical power system we still use today), for his inventions and work with light bulbs, radar, for his invention of remote control, and most importantly for demonstrating the transmission of electrical energy/power without wires. Ahead of his time is an understatement.

[2] https://electrical-engineering-portal.com/nikola-tesla-everything-is-the-light
[3] *Isis Unveiled*, by H. P. Blavatsky.
[4] https://electrical-engineering-portal.com/nikola-tesla-everything-is-the-light

[5] https://www.washingtonpost.com/archive/opinions/1984/10/21/the-cosmic-riddle-how-rocks-and-stars-became-flesh-and-blood/01e27297-4b84-4902-8d30-980c110ac865/

[6] *Carnal Thoughts*, by Vivian Sobchack.

[7] www.InfoVision-Academy.com

[8] *The Healing Power of Water* was his first book on this subject.

[9] JamesClear.com

[10] https://summitlighthouse.nl/karma-is-the-key/

[11] Ibid.

[12] Andre Bareau, *Die Religionen Indiens*, quoted in *The Encyclopedia of Eastern Philosophy and Religion*, by Ingrid Fischer-Schreiber, Franz-Karl Ehrhard, Kurt Friedrichs, and Michael S. Diener, page 175.

[13] https://eandt.theiet.org/content/articles/2019/04/quantum-for-dummies-the-basics-explained/

[14] https://m.facebook.com/TheChopraFoundation/photos/a.309821872414439/1284719588257991

[15] Gareth Cook, "Does Consciousness Pervade the Universe?" *Scientific American.* https://www.scientificamerican.com/article/does-consciousness-pervade-the-universe/

[16] https://en.wikipedia.org/wiki/Panpsychism

[17] https://en.wikipedia.org/wiki/Consciousness

[18] Kristof Koch, "What Is Consciousness?" *Nature.* https://www.nature.com/articles/d41586-018-05097-x

[19] https://youtu.be/dwnR39tgqZs

[20] https://www.teachthought.com/learning/8-types-of-imagination/

[21] https://blog.aboutmybrain.com/the-importance-of-imagination

[22] https://www.merriam-webster.com/dictionary/character

[23]https://josephsononbusinessethics.com/2015/02/character-what-is-it-and-why-is-it-important. Used with permission.

[24] Jason Evans. *Christianity 101 Unit 3.*

[25] Gary DiGrazia, Jr., 2010 posting on Quora.com

[26] https://www.quora.com/Is-it-possible-for-the-human-body-to-create-an-electromagnetic-field

[27] https://www.popularmechanics.com/culture/tv/a12520/4287442/

[28] https://www.youtube.com/watch?v=5BU7-lUk2iE

[29] https://en.wikipedia.org/wiki/Human_microbiome

[30] Sara Sandrini, Marwh Aldriwesh, Mashael Alruways, and Primrose Freestone. https://pubmed.ncbi.nlm.nih.gov/25792117/

[31] https://maglab.caltech.edu/human-magnetic-reception-laboratory

[32] https://www.ted.com/talks/jill_bolte_taylor_my_stroke_of_insight?

[33] https://abcnews.go.com/Health/elon-musk-unveils-brain-chip-implant-fitbit-skull/story?id=72703840

[34] https://en.wikipedia.org/wiki/Traffic_and_Environmental_Zone

[35] https://www.sciencealert.com/calculations-show-it-d-be-impossible-to-control-a-rogue-super-smart-ai

[36] https://mkomissarov.com/en/

[37] https://www.icuacademy.co.uk

[38] www.sehen-ohne-augen.de

[39] https://vibravision.com/

[40] Michael Sky, *Breathing.* 1990, Bear & Co., Santa Fe, NM. Used with permission.

[41] https://en.wikipedia.org/wiki/Herd_mentality

[42] https://en.wikipedia.org/wiki/Michael_D._Gershon

[43] Susan Jeffers, Ph.D. *Feel the Fear...and Do It Anyway.* 1987. Ballantine Books.

44 https://www.nhsinform.scot/healthy-living/mental-wellbeing/fears-and-phobias/ten-ways-to-fight-your-fears
45 Inner and Outer Worlds (2012 movie, available for purchase on YouTube)
46 https://en.wikipedia.org/wiki/Fractal
47 http://www.artandpopularculture.com/Fractals
48 https://findanyanswer.com/what-is-paisley-fabric-made-from
49 https://en.wikipedia.org/wiki/Holography
50

http://www.hrpub.org/download/20180730/IJRH2-19290514.pdf
51 https://www.fullcircle.sg/collections/sacred-geometry
52 Ryan Harris, *Neuroplasticity*, 2014. Createspace Publishing.
53 Tashira Tachi-ren with Archangel Ariel, *What is Lightbody?* 1999, New Leaf Distributing, Lithia Springs, GA. Used with permission.
54 Brian Scott, *The Reality Revolution*. 2020. Lioncrest Publishing.
55

https://en.wikipedia.org/wiki/Quantum_entanglement
56

https://www.youtube.com/watch?v=z2QVJbuMmEc